SINGULAR PASTS

SINGULAR PASTS

The "I" in Historiography

ENZO TRAVERSO

Translated by Adam Schoene

Columbia University Press

New York

Columbia University Press
Publishers Since 1893
New York   Chichester, West Sussex
cup.columbia.edu

Translation copyright © 2023 Columbia University Press
Passés singuliers: Le "je" dans l'écriture de l'histoire
copyright © Lux Éditeur 2020
Published by special arrangement with Lux Éditeur in conjunction
with their duly appointed agent 2 Seas Literary Agency

Library of Congress Cataloging-in-Publication Data
Names: Traverso, Enzo, author. | Schoene, Adam, translator.
Title: Singular pasts: the "I" in historiography / Enzo Traverso;
(translated from French by Adam Schoene).
Other titles: Passés singuliers. English
Description: New York: Columbia University Press, 2023. |
Includes bibliographical references and index.
Identifiers: LCCN 2022014173 (print) | LCCN 2022014174 (ebook) |
ISBN 9780231203982 (hardback) | ISBN 9780231203999
(trade paperback) | ISBN 9780231555319 (ebook)
Subjects: LCSH: Historiography. | Autobiography. | First person
narrative. | Self in literature. | History in literature. | Subjectivity. |
Subjectivity in literature. | Objectivity. | Objectivity in literature.
Classification: LCC D13.2 .T73513 2023 (print) |
LCC D13.2 (ebook) | DDC 907.2—dc23/eng/20220328
LC record available at https://lccn.loc.gov/2022014173
LC ebook record available at https://lccn.loc.gov/2022014174

Printed and bound by CPI Group (UK) Ltd, Croydon, CR0 4YY

Cover design: Chang Jae Lee
Cover image: Detail of *The Death of Marat*, by Jerome Martin
Langlois after the original by Jacques-Louis David,
© Château de Versailles, France/Bridgeman Images

CONTENTS

SINGULAR PASTS

INTRODUCTION

We never live only by our own efforts, we never live
only for ourselves; our most intimate, our most personal
thinking is connected by a thousand links with that of
the world.

— Victor Serge, *Memoirs of a Revolutionary*

THIS BOOK was born of a vague questioning that has grown and
become clearer in recent years, inspired by readings lacking sys-
tematic character and unmotivated by any professional project
or duty: books read out of curiosity, for pleasure, because reviews
had given me the desire to read them or because friends had
spoken to me of them; books that I have read with interest and
often enjoyed, which have helped me to think, have enlightened
me, have touched me, and offered the impression, at times, of
seeing the grain of the past, that is to say, of seeing human
beings in flesh and bone, beyond the concepts that are my working tools. They are history books, but also novels, autobiographies, or hybrid creations that mix different literary genres, and
some of them drew my admiration, but there remained something that troubled me. No singular works led to this perplexity: it arose from an ensemble of readings through a sort of accumulation effect.

The fact is simple: history is increasingly written in the first person, through the prism of the subjectivity of the author. If, in literature, this is an ancient phenomenon—one must think back only to Dante's *Divine Comedy*—it is different for history, where it is completely unprecedented. This invasive rise of the ego puzzles me. It questions my practices as a historian, but it also raises other deeper questions concerning the world in which we live. Is the era of the *selfie* impacting historical writing practices? Even before taking into consideration the methodological innovations that arise, we see this new place of subjectivity in anodyne details such as the growing tendency to feature the portrait of the author on the cover of certain books. This decision is not necessarily due to the "egotism" of writers—"my favorite subject, myself"—but rather to the new place occupied by subjectivity in our culture, and by extension, in a reified public sphere. I myself have experienced, on a very modest scale, this new display—or exhibition—of the self. A few years ago, I was amazed to find, when I received the translation of one of my books, that, instead of the usual biographical blurb, my face took up the entire back cover. When I inquired about the reasons for such a strange choice, my editor explained that it was the collection mock-up. A little later, I published a work on interwar Europe, the preface of which included some pages devoted to my "post-memory." I spoke of my hometown—a very ordinary little Italian town—and of the microcosm of memories, legends, and images that accompanied my adolescence and through which History with its capital *H*, once it became a local drama, was transmitted to my generation. I just wanted to explain how I learned, when I was still a teenager, of the events described and analyzed in my book, starting from the principle that for an author to present himself—to say from where he is speaking—is a form of intellectual honesty. I was surprised—and not always flattered—to see that, in a number of the countries where the book had been translated, the reviews lingered on the marginal autobiographical notes. A well-known Italian magazine asked my permission to publish the preface, and a large publishing house even suggested that I write a history of the 1970s from an autobiographical angle, disregarding the fact that I was only twenty years old in 1977 and that I played no major role in the events of the time. It all struck me as anecdotal and insignificant, even amusing, but I later realized that these were signs of a change in our relationship to the past.

At the turn of the twenty-first century, the autobiographies of historians multiplied. Jeremy D. Popkin and Jaume Aurell, the accredited analysts of this new literary genre, have identified several hundred over the past thirty years.[1] While affirming that a phenomenon of such magnitude deserves to be studied, they do not fail to point out its somewhat paradoxical character: generally, the life of a scholar consists of teaching courses and seminars, attending conferences, and holing oneself up in archives and libraries, which isn't exactly as thrilling as the adventures of a James Bond. Nevertheless, the pleasure that historians have taken in recounting their lives has spread. Until then, this self-reflective enjoyment had been reserved for a small minority of scholars aware of their celebrity and proud of the singular character of their careers. They belonged to an elite; they stood out from ordinary historians to become *memorialists*.[2] Edward Gibbon, Henry Adams, and later Benedetto

Croce and Friedrich Meinecke—the most recent is probably Eric J. Hobsbawm—all published their memories with the more or less explicit purpose of inscribing their lives in history.[3] This also applies to atypical autobiographies, written without the slightest intention of setting their authors up as models, but rather because they were aware of having become, through their work, the incarnation of a collective conscience. This is the case with the autobiographical fragments of Eduardo Galeano,[4] writer and essayist turned historian by transgressing his own vocation, to whom we owe one of the greatest works on the conquest of the New World, *The Open Veins of Latin America* (1971). Or the autobiography of Howard Zinn, written some fifteen years after the immense success of his *A People's History of the United States* (1980). In it he recounts his participation in World War II, his first job as a university professor in Atlanta, at the time of the struggle against racial segregation, then his activism against the Vietnam War, but beyond the memories of a historian he offers those of an activist.[5]

Memoirs, as Jean-Louis Jeannelle has shown, are born from the "dialectic between an individual destiny and the destiny of a community."[6] Those of statesmen almost always denote a desire to monumentalize their life; among historians, they express at least the awareness of having a place in the culture of a country or an era. Nowadays, however, this practice has spread to scholars who are totally unknown outside their discipline and who write autobiographies rather than memoirs. Their goal, in most cases, is not to erect a monument but to excavate within themselves so as to better understand their own intellectual trajectory or, more simply, to tell their life story.

This proliferation in the number of historian autobiographies is undoubtedly in part the reflection of a larger trend: the democratization of writing practices, and especially of self writing. The end of the intellectual elite's monopoly on writing—the nineteenth century was the age of combating illiteracy and the twentieth the age of the spread of reading; we entered that of the appropriation of writing by those who had been excluded until then—led ordinary women and men to tell their lives. The birth of the "history from below" is inseparable from the "autobiography from below," an extensive but marginal genre, which was formed and propagated in the shadows, outside consecrated press and publishing circuits. And the first to have understood the extraordinary richness of this vast textual landscape were indeed historians.

In Italy, many of them transcribed the testimonies of those who did not have access to writing. Danilo Montaldi was one of the first scholars to study the culture of the subaltern classes by attempting to reproduce their voices, in a literary form respectful of their language, hybrid and steeped in dialects. In his *Autobiografie della leggera* (1961), he featured the words of vagabonds, petty thugs, and prostitutes from the towns of the Po Valley,[7] thus painting a striking portrait of an engulfed world. In the wake of Jean Norton Cru, Antonio Gibelli reconstructed the history of the Great War through the voices of those who lived it low to the ground, in the trenches.[8] More recently, historians have studied this vast autobiographical production within the world of communist activists, where this practice was first used to select party executives but, in retrospect, reveals the trajectories of the lives of grassroots members.[9]

Mauro Boarelli studied the autobiographies of twelve hundred communist activists in Bologna, written between 1945 and 1956.[10] They describe a quite different landscape from that shown by traditional histories of communism, focused on the leaders, strategies, and collective action. Yet the memoirs of activists tell of their lives and describe the complex relationship that the popular classes had with high culture and the importance of writing and speaking in defining internal party hierarchies. To study the democratization of writing, historians had to make it into a research field. Although arising from the same process of democratizing self-writing, the autobiographies of historians and those of people belonging to the lower classes do not overlap. Nonetheless, there is a link between them, for it was only after studying the autobiographies of common people that "ordinary" historians began to tell their own lives.

In recent years, another threshold has been crossed: we have moved from historians' autobiographies to a new subjectivist form of history writing. Today, a growing number of works that are not autobiographies have an important homodiegetic dimension, as if history could not be written without exposing the interiority not only of those who make it but also, and above all, of those who write it. Neither history in the conventional sense of the term nor autobiography, this new hybrid genre has achieved considerable success. It transgresses traditions and goes beyond the literary canons by questioning certain fundamental and generally accepted premises of the historical discipline. It is this new place assigned to subjectivity in the writing of history and in the self-consciousness of historians that I will endeavor to study in the pages that follow. I would like to be clear: my intention is not to add a new stone to the already old edifice of anti-autobiographical literature, the origins of which go back at least to Pascal and his famous sentence "The self is hateful,"[11] which, much more than a simple joke, denoted real discomfort. In the autobiographical fragments that were used to compose *Berlin Chronicle* (1932), Walter Benjamin admitted that he had always adhered, as a critic, to "one little rule," simple, but scrupulously observed: "Never use the word 'I' except in letters." When asked to write columns on Berlin in the first person, he had to overcome a spontaneous reluctance: "It became suddenly clear that this subject, accustomed for years to waiting in the wings, would not so easily be summoned to the limelight."[12]

Autobiography is not a minor genre, with all due respect to Albert Thibaudet, who, in his essay on Gustave Flaubert, described it as "the most false" of self-disclosures, because it presents itself, at first glance, as "the most sincere" of them.[13] Nor a writer's ruse aimed, as Paul Valéry has suggested, to arouse curiosity by "unbuttoning" to give the impression of delivering intimacy.[14] A little earlier, in fin de siècle France, Ferdinand Brunetière's anti-autobiographical charge was much more violent. Although fiercely conservative, his attack could have been written today: "What are the causes of this sickly and monstrous development of the ego?" he wondered, lamenting that this hateful self has now conquered "the right to display itself in its glory and to stand in its insolence." And he continued, ruthlessly:

When we open a book, will it be to learn, as if we were foundlings, that the author had a father, brothers, a family; or the age that he is teething, how long his whooping cough lasted, the teachers he had in school, and how he did on his baccalaureate? Will we invite our novelists, as we used to do with our painters, to mirror themselves in their works, or to portray themselves in them with exactitude, for the instruction of posterity? And is it ultimately a tendency that we should encourage among them, that this infinite complacency for their notable person—without being wary that it is not also a form of the most impertinent disdain for everything that is not them?[15]

Even if it could be addressed to a number of contemporary authors, this severe indictment leads to rather poor conclusions. According to Brunetière, this "tendency of our authors to put themselves on stage" would only be the expression of their "fatuity" and "insignificance," of their dedication to write "locked up and as if imprisoned in the narrow circle of their egotism."[16] Everything considered, it is a myopic gaze. The results, as much literary as historiographical, of this writing, which is certainly centered on—but not necessarily locked within—the author's ego, can be remarkable. Sometimes regrettable, sometimes admirable, this emergence of the ego asks, above all, for explanation and critical interpretation.

"Novelist Narcissus" is no longer alone.[17] This literary figure, whose existence has been documented and studied for some time, now has at his side a "Historian Narcissus," much younger, but no less ambitious and creative.[18] Their ancestor appears in the third book of Ovid's *Metamorphoses*, where the poet is enchanted by his own image reflected in the crystal-clear water of a fountain. Charmed with himself, writes Ovid, to the point of becoming both the lover and the loved object, the desiring being and the object of his desire—"it was himself he loved"—he tries to possess his image, but this illusory effort leads him to his ruin, for he is ultimately swallowed up by the waters (3:407). Freud, and a good number of psychoanalysts in his wake, saw Narcissus as a neurotic figure, that of the subject who, unable to direct his libidinal energies outward, internalizes them in a sort of escape from reality by isolating and closing himself within.[19] He described a neurosis that undoubtedly affects many writers and historians, but he also simplified the complexity of the mythical character. Long before the father of psychoanalysis, Herman Melville had already given Narcissus the features of the universal. In this unfortunate hero, who, "because he could not grasp the tormenting, mild image he saw in the fountain, plunged into it and was drowned," the author of *Moby Dick* believed he had found the very source of history: "But that same image, we ourselves see in all rivers and oceans. It is the image of the ungraspable phantom of life; and this is the key to it all."[20]

The subjectivist historian, Historian Narcissus, resembles Melville's Narcissus more than Freud's. Instead of fleeing the world, he wants to explore it without losing sight of his own reflection, which life and history constantly send back to him. And this leads us, by analogy with Max Weber, to the notion of "inner-worldly" narcissism. In his most famous work, the German sociologist captures one of the features of the spirit of capitalism in "inner-worldly asceticism" (*innerweltlichen Askese*) that Protestantism—Calvin in particular—has opposed to mystical asceticism and that consists in seeking salvation through virtuous and rational action in society rather than by flight from the world.[21] Historian Narcissus arises from the desire to understand the past. It cannot therefore be reduced to a purely reflexive posture of self-contemplation and self-admiration, the ultimate spring of which, according to the Freudian definition, lies in the libido withdrawn from the outside world and brought to the subject own self (*ego-libido*). Historian Narcissus projects his energies outward, because his identity quest can only be completed through a long work of investigation of the past, a work recounted in the first person that allows him, after having questioned the life of others, to finally understand who he is and where he comes from.

If truth be told, Novelist Narcissus and Historian Narcissus are not to be juxtaposed with one another, as they tend to meet, and even to merge, into a hybrid figure, because, as we will see at the conclusion of these chapters, subjectivist historians do not hide their literary ambitions, while many novelists have begun writing like historians, exploring the world and producing works of "literary nonfiction." Like literary narcissism, historian narcissism calls for critique, while recognizing that its results are not negligible and sometimes even more remarkable than those of impersonal history.

Chapter One

WRITING IN THIRD PERSON

HISTORIANS BEGAN writing in the third person as early as antiquity, when there were no distinct boundaries between history, poetry, tragedy, and eloquence, these being, to borrow the words of Nicole Loraux, "institutions of speech anchored in the city-state."[1]

Despite having participated in the Peloponnesian Wars, first as an Athenian general then as an exile, Thucydides did not wish to give his own testimony of the event. He wanted to write as a historian and reconstruct the conflict through objective description of the facts, an approach that required third-person narration. And so, he pointed out, he did not write *History of the Peloponnesian War* as a poet, because he did not wish to embellish the events of that time. He also distanced himself from the "prose chroniclers"—his designation for those annalists of the sixth and fifth centuries BC—whose stories were "written more to please the ear than to serve the truth,"[2] and who spoke of facts that were not verifiable and therefore could not make any claims to authenticity. His method was different because his account was grounded in "the clearest evidence available."[3] He carried out "the greatest possible rigor in pursuing every detail" for events that he had himself lived through just as he did for those of which he only had indirect knowledge. He thus asked the indulgence of readers who may have found "the lack of a romantic element in [his] story" as rigorously and factually reconstructing the past demanded an impersonal narrative voice.[4] According to the classicist Luciano Canfora, it was the sudden introduction of an "I" in chapters 25 and 26 of book 6 that allowed Xenophon to identify himself as having completed Thucydides' text. The transition from third- to first-person narration also served to authenticate the veracity of his account through his status as an eyewitness: "I lived through the whole of the war, studying it with mature perception and in the intellectual pursuit of an accurate understanding of events."[5] Hence, Thucydides' successor chose a double narrative register to articulate both the historian's impersonal narrative voice (Thucydides) and an eyewitness account written in the first person (Xenophon himself).

From the birth of modern historiography as purported scientific discipline, toward the end of the eighteenth century, writing in the third person has been one of its cardinal rules. In fact, until relatively recent times, it has been assumed to be unquestionable. The premise is quite simple: conceived as a rational operation of factual reconstruction and contextualized chronological description of past events, history implies a distance, a looking outward, which the impersonal narrative alone could assure. To be meticulously rebuilt and understood to its greatest extent, the past must be relieved from any depth of feeling that envelops it, an essential task that only the external observer—chronologically and even psychologically detached from the facts they describe—can accomplish. Leopold Ranke, the founder of the German historical school, envisaged history as a convergence between science (*Wissenschaft*) and self-education (*Bildung*), between scrupulous research methodology and the pedagogical mission implicit in any effort to produce knowledge. At once occupation and calling—two notions that come together in the German concept of profession (*Beruf*) per the Weberian definition for scientific work—history could not, he argued, be recounted subjectively or, worse, intimately.[6] While the nation-states seemed to embody its accomplishment in Hegelian terms, history becomes a necessarily impersonal, objective, collective, and public narrative, sometimes at risk of being mistaken for a notarial deed, a report ready to be archived. Conceived as a scientific discourse, history codified its rules by assimilating and merging procedures put in place by other disciplines, notably the rhetoric of law (an art of persuasion based on the exhibition of evidence) and the experimental practices of medicine (a diagnosis based on empirical observations). Above all, knowledge of the past involved its objectification and its rational description in accordance with a vision that has only recently been called into question with the advent of the linguistic turn in the humanities and social sciences.

Even the irruption of memory in the realm of historiography did not alter these principles. Attentive to its eminently subjective nature, historians have always treated it as a source like any other, to be validated, corroborated, and compared. In short, the historian approached memory as a new *object* of investigation. In his introduction to *Realms of Memory* (1984), Pierre Nora reaffirms an almost ontological distinction—previously observed by Maurice Halbwachs in the 1920s—between memory and history by emphasizing their constitutive dichotomy: memory is made of recollections while history is founded on sources; memory is the presence of a still living past while history supposes that past to be absent, cold, and long dead; memory is the subjective perception of a past that history deems concretized and sealed. In order to write a history of collective memory, scholars must locate themselves on the side of the former, not the latter. For them—we should emphasize this point—memory is but one of many sources that clutter their workshop among documents, archival materials, texts, letters, images, films, and all manner of material objects. Should they come across or gather memories, these sources must be verified, deciphered, contextualized, and interpreted. That is to say, they "reify" them.[7] They cannot replace them or mix them with their own memories, even if they feel tempted to do so. The oral history expert must collect voices of actors of the past with the respect, humility, and care that these eyewitness accounts demand, all the while maintaining the critical distance needed to scrupulously verify the correlation between the accounts and facts. In certain cases—as long as one is not confronted by liars—it is precisely the gap between testimony and established fact, once analyzed and explained, that has allowed knowledge of the past to progress.[8] The historian's objective is to understand what has happened and not to reveal the extent to which discovery of the past affects them or helps them probe the depths of the soul.

Interrogating the past through the lens of their own memories is not the task of the historian, but rather that of the memorialist. Anyone who feels this urge would do better to satisfy it in a location as discreet as the pages of a diary. This is why Tocqueville, author of *The Old Regime and the Revolution* (1856), envisaged his recollections of 1848 as a sort of "mirror," in which he could examine his contemporaries and himself, and not as a tableau intended to be shown to the public. This collection of observations was of a strictly private nature and could only become a matter of record posthumously. His friends were not permitted to read it, and it was only published in 1893:

> these recollections shall be a relaxation of the mind rather than a contribution to literature. I write them for myself alone. They shall be a mirror in which I will amuse myself in contemplating my contemporaries and myself; not a picture painted for the public. My most intimate friends shall not see them, for I wish to retain the liberty of depicting them as I shall depict myself, without flattery. I wish to arrive truly at the secret motives which have caused them, and me, and others to act; and, when discovered, to reveal them here. In a word, I wish this expression of my recollections to be a sincere one; and to effect this, it is essential that it should remain absolutely secret.[9]

Since writing in the third person had become a shared and unquestionable rule within the discipline of history, writing one's own memories was seen by the historian as a sort of transgression. Jeremy D. Popkin stresses that history "requires

considerable sublimation of the self," which returns to a definition of autobiography as the expression of a (more or less) conscious desire to violate this fixed norm.[10] In an age when positivism triumphed, French historians openly aired their
repugnance for individuality in an ostentatious manner. Gabriel
Monod, founder of the *Revue historique,* and his followers—
notably Numa Fustel de Coulanges and Charles Seignobos—
conceived of their discipline as a sort of radical asceticism that
completely erased their subjectivity. Charles Péguy—one of the
first writers who refused to distinguish between history and
literature—deplored this posture. In his eyes, it consisted in
being unaware of the present—the surroundings of the historian himself—and lauding this ignorance as a virtue, if not "the
very condition for accessing knowledge of the past."[11] To qualify as objective and sufficiently distant from the events in question, historical narration had to be anonymous and the historian undetectable lest they make their presence known in any
way.

Throughout the second half of the nineteenth century, the
institutionalization of history—now viewed as a scientific discipline ultimately emancipated from literature—supposed the
expulsion of the "self." As Ivan Jablonka explains, the "I" had
to be progressively submitted to an objective paradigm borrowed from the natural sciences—for which Claude Bernard
had laid the foundation in his *Introduction to the Study of Experimental Medicine* (1865)—that required a radical separation
between, on the one hand, observation and analysis of events
and, on the other hand, the subject that carried them out. By
erasing their subjectivity, the historian hid behind an "absence-
omnipresence" that gave the illusion of having established an

objective, neutral narrative; to express themself, Jablonka concludes, like a sort of "Author-God."[12] The subjectivity on display could only belong to actors of the past. As explained in his major works from *The People* (1846) to *The History of the French Revolution* (1850–1853), Jules Michelet's ambition was to restore and revive the past with its emotions, passions, hopes, tragedies, and urges. Meticulously reconstructing events based on his exploration of sources was equally essential to such a task as identifying empathetically with the actors of a given time. In his eyes, the historian's aim was the "resurrection" of the past; he wished to resuscitate that which had happened by penetrating the minds of those who had participated in making it happen. Beneath its apparent coldness, the archival document hid the secret of life:

> These papers and parchments, so long deserted, desired no better than to be restored to the light of the day; yet are they not papers, but lives of men, of provinces, and of nations. . . . Softly, my dear friends, let us proceed in order, if you please. All of you have your claim on history. . . . And, as I breathed on their dust, I saw them rise up. They raised from the sepulcher, one the hand, the other the head, as in the Last Judgement of Michelangelo, or in the Dance of Death. This galvanic dance, which they performed around me, I have essayed to reproduce in this work.[13]

According to François Hartog, Michelet's approach is, in many ways, the antithesis of that of Fustel de Coulanges: rather than conceal himself, he tries to commune with the dead. Fustel, Hartog writes, "strives to not exist, negating himself in order to know the past; the other [Michelet] creates a contract with absence and becomes a visitor to the dead. . . . Here you have two types of absence, two relationships with time, two strategies for acquiring knowledge, two ways of writing history. Like Péguy, Michelet sides with memory, Fustel with history."[14] Citing his *Journal,* Christophe Prochasson points out that Michelet is the inventor of the "me-history" (*moi-histoire*).[15] Departing from different premises, proponents of German historicism also consider identification with actors of the past to be a necessary condition for reconstructing a historical account. Ranke calls it "empathy" (*Einfühlung*), and Dilthey "lived experience" (*Erlebnis*).[16] For Michelet as for Dilthey, this methodology allows the historian to penetrate the mental and emotional world of a bygone society in order to understand it. However, it certainly does not authorize the historian to replace their own individuality with the mental universe conjured: the "empathy" they recommend is not a dialogue between interchangeable interlocutors. These two historians do not so much call the third-person historical narrative into question as they do problematize it.

This tension between the emergence of a new subjectivity and the positivist imperative of an impersonal narrative spans the entire nineteenth century. The historiographical debates are but one expression among many. The same epoch also saw literature fracture around this new "ego." Researchers have traced its appearance to Jean-Jacques Rousseau's *Confessions* (1782), the first modern autobiography. François-René de Chateaubriand, Alphonse de Lamartine, George Sand, and Alexandre Dumas follow his example, but run up against resistance and misunderstanding. For Chateaubriand, eloquence too often supersedes sincerity, and his *Memoirs from Beyond the Grave* (1849–1850) are often considered the outpourings of a senile Narcissus. Gérard de Nerval was the first poet to put his own dreams on paper and to transform his illness into a source of aesthetic creation, a half a century before psychoanalysis and surrealism. Yet his autobiographical texts are seen as the foolishness of a madman, more interesting for medicine than literature.

The artistic potential of the subjectivity of writers would not be fully recognized until the advent of the avant-garde at the beginning of the twentieth century.[17] Naturalism came to an end, realism in painting fizzled out, and photography was emancipated from these original aesthetic models. Such shifts mark a break in the representation of the real and disrupt the chronological unity of literary narratives by allowing the author's subjectivity to come through alongside that of their characters. Marcel Proust, Franz Kafka, Joseph Conrad, Italo Svevo, Luigi Pirandello, and James Joyce exemplify this irruption of modernism in literature by transforming the novel into a sort of "interior monologue;" T. S. Eliot and Ezra Pound will do much the same with poetry and Bertolt Brecht with theater. However, during the "long nineteenth century," from Benjamin Constant to Proust, writers are obliged to remind their critics that the "I" in their novels does not make them autobiographies nor does it challenge their standing as "works of imagination."[18] As for historians, they remain impermeable to these literary quarrels around the "I." What interested the author of the *Confessions*, the book that set up the autobiographical paradigm for the nineteenth century, "is not the historical truth, but the emotion of a conscience letting the past emerge in it."[19] Autobiography thus does not yet concern historians.

Almost a century after Michelet, Siegfried Kracauer reaffirms that it is the historian's job to "resuscitate" the dead. For him, history is at once a multiform reality and a narration, an ensemble of facts and their representation. In its capacity as a retrospective creation that inevitably entails some amount of subjectivity, history cannot be assimilated to the natural sciences and without question possesses a literary or even artistic dimension. In other words, historians are neither naturalists nor novelists, even if, like the former, they work with material that has not been invented and if, like the latter, they *write*. That is, they transform this material into a narrative fabric, into a plot. Like Orpheus, Kracauer explains in *History: The Last Things Before the Last* (1969), "the historian must descend into the nether world to bring the dead back to life" and while this perilous experience may become an artistic accomplishment, they must respect the rules if they wish the work to remain "history."[20] Kracauer concludes that their art "remains anonymous because it primarily shows in historian's capacity for self-effacement and self-expansion and in the import of his diagnostic probings."[21]

For those historians who accept the principle of causal determinism, impersonal writing is a dogma. According to François Simiand and Karl Lamprecht, the goal of historical science is not to recover the uniqueness of a life, but rather its inscription in a landscape and temporality of constraints, repetition, and conformity. What is unique, Simiand writes, "has neither cause nor scientific explanation."[22] This "scientific" interpretation of the past is antipodal to the meeting of the subjectivity of the historian and that of historical actors. Postwar structuralist historiography, the age of the "death of the subject," will abandon the most radical forms of this determinism but will not renounce the sacred norm of impersonal writing. For Fernand Braudel, author of *The Mediterranean* (1949), history is an "anonymously human" process in which living beings are thrust into vast spaces and shaped by stratified demographic, geographic, economic, and mental structures.[23] It is Louis Althusser, a Marxist philosopher, who will take it upon himself to codify this concept with his well-known definition of history as "process without a subject."[24] Stressing that a "subject" only exists within a social space and an inherited habitus, Pierre Bourdieu will in turn denounce what he called the "biographical illusion," offering the metaphor of a trip on the subway: "trying to understand a career or a life as a unique and self-sufficient series of successive events without any other link than association with a 'subject' . . . is almost as absurd as trying to make sense of a trip on the metro without taking the structure of the network into account, meaning the matrix of objective relations between the different stations."[25] Entangled in the complex fabric of social, economic, cultural, and symbolic relations, subjectivity disappears.

Chapter Two

THE PITFALLS OF OBJECTIVITY

THE MOST striking example of third-person narration is probably *History of the Russian Revolution* (1930–1932), which Leon Trotsky wrote while on the small Turkish island of Prinkipo (today called Büyükada), near Istanbul, shortly after his expulsion from Stalin's Soviet Union. Not wanting to deliver a testimony of a historical event in which he had played a crucial role by giving his account the color of lived experience, he decided to write as a historian, using the largest documentation then available on this event, published by the Moscow Institute for the History of Revolution. He therefore writes about himself in the third person, calling himself by name and placing himself on the same level as the other actors of his sumptuous historical tableau. He does not hide the epistemological advantages conferred by his status as protagonist, and implicitly recognizes that his work is nourished by and filled with his memories, but he insists on the objective character of his reconstruction, a story that is scrupulously corroborated by sources and keeps every individualistic temptation at a distance. Rich and deceiving at the same time, subjective, limited, and one-sided, his memory certainly irrigates his work, he honestly admits, but he never used it without first submitting it to a very strict verification. He denies any claim to "treacherous impartiality," but at the same time assures that his research is grounded on his "scientific conscientiousness," that is, on "an honest study of the facts, a determination of their real connections, an exposure of the causal laws of their movement."[1] In his eyes, this is the only "historical objectivity" possible. In his book, he underscores that he does not want to show off or give his choices a retrospective justification. Rather, he tries to distance himself from the events he describes and to give a critical interpretation of the role he played in them. Obviously, he cannot paint his self-portrait. He cannot try to describe his own personality, as he did for many other figures in his historical fresco, from Tsar Nicholas II to Alexander Kerensky, from Menshevik leaders like Julius Martov and Fedor Dan to Bolshevik leaders themselves, beginning with V. I. Lenin, Grigory Zinoviev, and Lev Borisovich Kamenev.

In his preface to the second volume, Trotsky cites Dickens and Proust, emphasizing that telling the past does not mean anesthetizing it: laughter and tears cannot be erased from the collective dramas that punctuate the movement of history. The state of mind, moods, passions, and feelings of individuals, classes, and mass movements deserve the same attention with which Proust probes, over hundreds of pages, the mind and psychology of his characters. An accurate account of the

Napoleonic battles, Trotsky adds, should go beyond the geometry of the camps, beyond the rationality and effectiveness of the generals' strategic and tactical choices. This account should also take into account the misunderstood orders, the inability of the generals to read a map, the panic and colic of fear that gripped the soldiers and officers before the attack.[2] Unlike Winston Churchill, who does not hide his contempt for professional historians—a category of human beings that he classifies well below statesmen and the military—and presents the six volumes of his history of the Second World War as a "personal narrative,"[3] Trotsky wants to be recognized as a writer and especially as a historian, which implies an account in the third person.

This posture is part of a more general trend. Twenty years earlier, Lord Acton, who edited *The Cambridge Modern History*, a monumental thirteen-volume work (1902–1912), asked its authors to write their chapters in a totally impersonal form. As he noted in a letter to the heads of this editorial enterprise, the reader must be unable to say "where the Bishop of Oxford [Stubbs] laid down his pen and whether Fairbairn or Gasquet, Liebermann or Harrison took it up."[4] For several decades, the mere mention of subjectivity inevitably aroused the greatest skepticism among British and American historians. Against the grain, and a good fifteen years ahead of Pierre Nora, Lewis Perry Curtis edited in the 1970s *The Historian's Workshop*, a collection of autobiographies of historians: thirty-seven of the fifty-two scholars he asked to collaborate refused, judging the enterprise more than suspect. One of them was offended, "both from the scholarly and the aesthetic point of view," by a request that revealed to his eyes the pernicious influence of psychoanalysis on the historical discipline.[5]

It goes without saying that this tendency to fetishize historical objectivity was often nothing but an alibi that served to hide shameful intentions. During the 1950s, in the Federal Republic of Germany (FRG), when many former high-ranking Nazi officials were being rehabilitated in silence and the Holocaust obscured—what was called not without cynicism to "master" or "overcome the past" (*Vergangenheit Bewältigung*)—Jewish scholars were often viewed with suspicion by their colleagues. People like Armin Mohler, former secretary of Ernst Jünger and historian of the conservative revolution, and Martin Broszat, former member of the Hitler Youth, freshly recruited from within the Institute of Contemporary History in Munich, believed that Jewish scholars working on the history of National Socialism were not objective enough. According to Mohler and Broszat, the work of Leon Poliakov and Joseph Wulf—the first to extensively document Nazi crimes and the Holocaust in postwar Germany—was vitiated by nefarious polemical intent and imbued with bitterness and resentment. This bias, they claimed, made them more apt to work in a denazification commission than to enrich objective knowledge of Hitlerism. Their anti-Nazi arguments, Broszat explained, propagated the danger of an emotional approach that could not result in true "rational conviction." His conclusion was even more severe: "When elevated to a principle, bitterness and sarcasm" could "be no help in historically deciphering the phenomenon of National Socialism."[6]

Some thirty years later, Broszat espoused a substantially similar position in his correspondence with Saul Friedländer. Against the "mythical form of this remembrance" specific to victims, he championed the scientific processes of historicization (*Historisierung*) of National Socialism which, in basing itself on criteria of "objectification" and "explanatory distancing," exceeded the limits of a simple moral condemnation, understandable, but sterile.[7] In his reply, Friedländer noted that Jewish and German historians had a different "choice of focus" regarding the Nazi past and that a "fusion of horizons" was not yet in sight.[8] This observation led him to recognize the subjectivity of the scholar in the writing of history and to underline the hypocrisy of the scientific mask adopted by Broszat: why would a representative of the Hitler Youth generation be more "objective" than a Jewish person? Historians, he added, "are inextricably caught in a web composed of personal recollections, general social conditioning, acquired professional knowledge, and attempts at critical distancing."[9] However, lucid as it was, this focus neither contested the principle, according to which the historiography of the Nazi era had to adhere to criteria "as strictly scientific as that of any other period,"[10] nor the requirement of writing in the third person, as much for conceptual history as for narrative history.

In transforming his own experience of the war into an "objective" understanding of Nazi Germany, Broszat gave in to a widely shared illusion. As part of the *Historikerstreit*, the quarrel of German historians over the singularity of the Holocaust, Andreas Hillgruber very candidly wrote that historians of

World War II must take into account the suffering of the German civilian population and understand the desperate efforts of the Wehrmacht soldiers to defend it against the fierceness and devastating vengeance of the Red Army.[11] Jürgen Habermas pointed out to him that without the "heroic resistance" of German soldiers on the Eastern Front, the Nazi extermination camps could not have functioned through January of 1945.[12] The account of the war proposed by Hillgruber in his book *Zweierlei Untergang* (1986) was the expression of a mental disposition quite common until the 1980s. The myth of scientific objectivity, cultivated for decades by the historiography of Western Germany, actually served to camouflage the subjectivity of a generation of scholars who had waged war, had been involved in the Nazi regime and mobilized an arsenal of well-established positivist arguments in order to justify, in a more or less conscious way, their apologetic aims. This kind of "historical objectivity" was only the facade of a national unconscious haunted by the ghosts of the past.

West German scholars were, however, not the only ones to fall into the trap of their subjectivity. One of the most important postwar historians, George L. Mosse, saw fit to include, in a pioneering essay on fascism, this strange comparison between Mussolini and Hitler: "The Duce showed more human dimensions than the Führer," he asserted, before adding that "Mussolini had no Auschwitz."[13] This comparison of the character of the two dictators arouses some perplexity. In his memoirs, published shortly before his death, Mosse gives us the key to explaining his complacency toward the Duce. In 1936, as we can read in *Confronting History* (2000), George, still an adolescent, was traveling to Italy with his mother when Mussolini and Hitler signed the Rome-Berlin Axis. Fearing that this political turn might lead to their expulsion, his mother wrote to Mussolini, who immediately assured her of his protection, adding that they could stay in the peninsula as long as they wished. The Duce had not forgotten the help that George's father, Hans Lachmann-Mosse, a German press magnate under the Prussian Empire and the Weimar Republic, had given him when he broke with the Socialist Party at the beginning of the Great War. This episode, writes Mosse, "throws light on Mussolini's character, at least upon his sense of gratitude."[14] So be it, but it is highly unlikely that a similar anecdote could be told by an Ethiopian or Libyan historian. One could also say that, in the same year of 1936, the directives, telegrams, and letters in which Mussolini ordered or approved the gas bombings and the other massacres committed by the Italian army in Ethiopia also shed light on his personality, a much darker light. Like other tyrants, Mussolini could be generous and cruel at the same time. Historians should therefore not draw general conclusions based on one-sided sources, much less their own memories or sympathies.

The part of subjectivity inherent in any writing of history was recognized late and often discreetly hidden. In many battles for the defense of historical truth, it would even have been unwelcome. To restore the honor of Captain Alfred Dreyfus, for example, it was necessary to prove that the accusations against him were false. And it is in the name of knowledge acquired and of an objective reality that has been repeatedly attested that Holocaust denial has been rejected. One of the most effective responses to Robert Faurisson's denial theses came from one of his former disciples, Jean-Claude Pressac, who, deeply convinced that the gas chambers were a myth, tried to prove it before facing reality and writing a well-documented essay on their origins and technical operation.[15] A number of historians who could hardly be accused of naive positivism have written essays on themes that directly and closely affected them and have chosen to write in the third person so as not to expose themselves to the accusation of subjectivism. In 1958, Pierre Vidal-Naquet, then a young Hellenist at the start of his career, published *L'affaire Audin*, adding to his name the mention "history specialist" (*agrégé d'histoire*). The official version of the disappearance of the young mathematician from Algiers Maurice Audin was a blatant lie, and he held to proving it with the expertise and carefulness of a historian.[16] Years later, he revealed in his memoirs the subjective sources of his "Dreyfusard" commitment against the Algerian War: the legacy of his parents deported and murdered at Auschwitz, the fervent republicanism of his father, and the fact—in his eyes simply unbearable—that French soldiers could inflict torture with impunity in Algeria as the Gestapo had done in France fifteen years earlier. In 1958, it was first necessary to demonstrate that power was lying; personal considerations would only have weakened his argument.

Thirty years later, it was as a historian that Carlo Ginzburg wrote *The Judge and the Historian* (1991).[17] He mobilized his knowledge of the Inquisition to prove that the trial continued against the former left-wing leader Adriano Sofri, accused of having ordered the murder of a Milan police chief during the lead years, was based only on speculation. Ideological arguments had replaced the old theological griefs, but the guilt of the accused was assumed a priori and therefore no longer needed to be proven. What Ginzburg convincingly demonstrated, on the contrary, was the inquisitorial staging of the trial against Sofri.[18] Honestly, he acknowledged his desire to prove the innocence of a friend, but if he had devoted a chapter to telling the story of their friendship, his whole argument would have come off less solid and less credible. His essay was not a testament to loyalty but aimed to unveil the gears of judicial persecution. In the same period, Claudio Pavone renewed the study of the Italian Resistance by reinterpreting it, beyond its canonical reading as a struggle for national liberation, as a class war as well, and above all as a "civil war."[19] He did not hide his participation in this war as a young antifascist activist—he spent a year in prison—but he did not write as a witness. Probing and analyzing the ethics of the Resistance required a critical distance that he did not consider compatible with testimony, much less with first-person writing.

All these examples show that, until very recent times, considering the subjectivity of the actors of the past always meant, for historians, an effort to remove—or at least to master—their own subjectivity. Even without denying it, they wished to control its consequences, to avoid harmful interferences and doubts about their objectivity. To many scholars, these concerns appear today as an obsolete vestige.

Chapter Three

EGO-HISTORY

THE FIRST signs of a shift appeared in the 1980s. At the beginning, there was a spectacular rise in studies of memory and the linguistic turn, which brought the questioning of identity into the humanities and social sciences. This coincided, on the political level, with the neoconservative turn embodied by Ronald Reagan and Margaret Thatcher: as public discourse focused on victims and human rights, historians began to abandon the analytical categories that had dominated the two preceding decades, especially those of class and collective action. With the fading of the great structuralist wave, the subject was coming back with force and reclaiming its rights. At the end of the decade, the fall of communism tipped the world into the twenty-first century, deeply shaking all its traditional identity benchmarks. The return of subjectivity also reflected this disorientation and entry into a world that previous interpretive keys no longer allowed us to understand. In 1979, Lawrence Stone published a noted article in which he announced, as a visionary, a "return to narrative": without calling into question the achievements of their discipline—notably its analytical character—historians rediscovered a taste for narration.[1]

In 1987, three years after inaugurating his major historiographical project on *Realms of Memory*, Pierre Nora gathered essays of "ego-history" by seven French scholars in a collection. The title was evocative, but, by his claims, the book was not very popular. It foreshadowed a trend that had not yet taken form. In the introduction, he rightly presented this enterprise as "a laboratory experiment in which historians attempt to turn into historians of themselves."[2] Of course, this did not mean revealing their private lives; it was more about the reconstruction of their academic trajectories, the exploration of their personal workshops, their intellectual customs, and their methodological choices, thus encouraging them to reconsider their careers and their works, which could prove fruitful. In order to avoid misunderstandings, Nora set limits upon this exercise: "These are not phony literary autobiographies, pointless intimate confessions, abstract professions of faith, or attempts at basic psychoanalysis."[3]

Unlike his nineteenth-century predecessors who tended to hide behind their archival files, or even "to hide their personality behind their knowledge," explained Nora, the contemporary historian now had to be ready to "admit there is a close and quite intimate link between themselves and their work." It was still just a hypothesis, a path to explore, but it had to be tried. This self-awareness was basically a safer and more effective "shelter" than conventional oaths of objectivity. The merits of the enterprise were evident: "The unveiling and analysis of existential involvement, rather than moving away from some impartial investigation, becomes instead an instrument for improving understanding."[4] The goal was not therefore to question the principle of objectivity, which remained at the heart of the discipline, but rather to note that historical objectivity required mature scholars aware of their personal involvement, capable of seeing themselves in the mirror amidst their work, and warned of the naive and illusory character of historiographical positivism. The project was ambitious, nonetheless, since Nora defined it as the elaboration of "a genre: ego-history, a new genre for a new period of historical consciousness."[5]

The *Essais d'ego-histoire* bring together texts by Maurice Agulhon, Pierre Chaunu, Georges Duby, Raul Girardet, Jacques Le Goff, Michelle Perrot, and René Rémond. In the 1980s, feminism certainly had a history, but gender parity had not yet entered into academic mores. The creation of this collection was no easy task, since there were many refusals, as Nora himself notes in his preface, even if nobody denied "the methodological interest of the proposal." For many historians, writing in the first person meant breaking a taboo. Paul Veyne—who would later write his memoirs—explained his refusal as such: "I cannot; and it is not for lack of trying."[6] Future memorialists such as Pierre Vidal-Naquet and Annie Kriegel also refused. After beginning his text in the third person, by the same token, Pierre Goubert gave up. Recently, Patrick Boucheron found, at the Institute for Contemporary Publishing Archives (IMEC), a first version of Georges Duby's essay, dated 1983. It is significantly different from the one published four years later, and, notably, it is written in the third person. This is how it starts: "In the summer of 1914, a few days before the general mobilization, Georges Duby's parents celebrated their marriage. Their only child was born on October 7, 1919, in Paris, in the 10th arrondissement. The father was 36 years old, the mother 29."[7] The style is refined, literary, and enjoyable to read. Far from the bursts of intelligence, passion, erudition, and critical thinking that fill the pages of *History Continues* (1991), which deals with the profession of the historian, this first essay on ego-history seems insipid: the polite, detached narrative, a bit bootlicking and self-satisfied with a brilliant academic career.[8] Fascinated from early on by Marc Bloch's *The Royal Touch: Monarchy and Miracles in France and England* and *Feudal Society*, he tells how this reading "unintentionally made him into a medievalist."[9] In the late 1930s, G.D.—as he calls himself throughout the text—would have settled nicely in Besançon: "He liked the city, simple, robust, devoid of bourgeois affectation."[10] The essay ends with his accession to the Collège de France thanks to the intervention in his favor by Paul Lemerle and Fernand Braudel. "G.D. was not without astonishment at the grace which the institute bestowed upon him in welcoming him," he writes with a very bourgeois preciosity, concluding with an equally conventional admission of modesty: "Very sensitive to this kind of honors, yet he is sometimes surprised to hold for another the one spoken of around him by pronouncing his name."[11] It gives the impression, at moments, of reading Voltaire's *Mémoires* (1776), also written in the third person: "The King of Prussia thus called Mr. Voltaire to him."[12]

Visibly disappointed with this first version, a CV in literary form, and "fearing to appear affected," Duby decided to rewrite his text in the first person, but not without warning the reader first. He would not tell his life story in it: "I will only show part of me in this ego-history. The *ego-laborer*, if you will, or the *ego-faber*."[13] He would not say anything about what he liked, would not speak, for example, of his passion for the theater or for music, to the point of underscoring the censorship he imposed on himself: "It is quite evident that the essential here is silent." He warned the readers that they would only find his "public life" there, and even advised them to "cast a wary gaze" on what would follow. Despite this admission of modesty and self-censorship, Duby wrote a much more lively and personal text. However, he could not help but express his mistrust of the exercise he had just completed in his conclusion. His dissatisfaction was not so much about his text or his accomplishments; it was due to his skepticism toward the very possibility of historians writing their own history. The "new genre" that Nora called for did not arouse his enthusiasm. He does not feel that "the historian is better placed than anyone to explore the memories that concern him" and calls upon the intransigence of posterity: "If by chance someone later seeks to inquire about what was in France, in the second third of the twentieth century, the profession of the historian, may he severely criticize this testimony."[14] A refusal, therefore, to deliver his private life as well as a failure of an attempt at an intellectual self-portrait.

■ ■ ■

Pierre Nora probably did not imagine that his "laboratory experiment" simply announced an autobiographical wave. Even without doing an inventory, as Jeremy Popkin and Jaume Aurell have attempted, one might sketch its typology by distinguishing four main categories. The first includes works in which the authors recount their lives, both public and private, bringing together intimate moments and professional experiences (Benedict Anderson, Saul Friedländer, Peter Gay, Eric J. Hobsbawm, Tony Judt, Mario Isnenghi, Walter Laqueur, George L. Mosse, Pierre Nora, Paul Veyne, and Eli Zaretsky).[15] The second gathers the autobiographies written as stories of oneself—Aurell calls them "monographic approaches to the self"[16]—based on carefully verified sources and personal archives, in which intimacy coexists with a presentation of the work accomplished, all supported by a rich apparatus of bibliographic notes (Annie Kriegel and Pierre Vidal-Naquet).[17] Vidal-Naquet's memoirs, which are based, beyond his own memories, on his father's letters and diary, describe the method. As he specifies in the foreword to the first volume, it is "a history book as much as a memory book, a history book of which I am both the author and the object."[18]

The third category includes autobiographies that, centered on an intellectual trajectory, explain certain methodological choices and develop a self-reflexive approach on the transformations that have affected historiography itself (Georges Duby, Geoff Eley, Sheila Fitzpatrick, Tulio Halperín Donghi, Raul Hilberg, Dominick LaCapra, Emmanuel Le Roy Ladurie, Gérard Noiriel, Zeev Sternhell, and others).[19] They can take the form of an intellectual fresco, describe the birth of a historian's vocation, or retrace a singular itinerary, impervious to both external fashions and academic conformism (Hilberg). They shape a particular genre that Carl E. Schorske calls the "professional self-portrait,"[20] which, as Eley underscores, avoids the pitfalls of total self-referentiality.[21]

Finally, the fourth group is made up of autobiographies anchored in foundational historical experiences such as wars, genocides, or revolutions, which have deeply marked both collective and individual life. This is the case with the autobiographies generated by the involvement of their authors in World War II (Paul Fussell, Richard Pipes, and Fritz Stern),[22] the Holocaust (Friedländer's first self-portrait),[23] or the revolts of the 1960s and 1970s (Anna Bravo, Giovanni De Luna, Luisa Passerini, Sheila Rowbotham, Benjamin Stora).[24] Some texts are unclassifiable, for example, *Landscape for a Good Woman* by Carolyn Steedman (1986). Anticipating by several decades a trend that is now widespread, Steedman weaves biography and autobiography into the same story, her own story and that of her mother, by introducing first-person writing into a period painting that depicts, according to the methods of British social history, the life of the working classes of south London in the 1950s and 1960s.[25] In most cases, however, these autobiographies were written on the fringes of a scholarly work carefully adhering to the norm of third-person narrative. In short, these were authorized "transgressions," more or less recognized as such. If we attempt a comparison with literature and philosophy, we could say that these personal narratives occupy, in the pathways of their authors, an isolated and singular position, a bit like the *Memoirs of a Dutiful Daughter* by Simone de Beauvoir (1958), *The Words* by Jean-Paul Sartre (1963), and, more recently, *Autoritratto nello studio* by Giorgio Agamben (2017).[26]

While there are several studies on female autobiographical writing,[27] feminist historians who have chosen to express themselves in the first person (Anna Bravo, Luisa Passerini, Sheila Rowbotham, Carolyn Steedman) remain few in number. The fundamental place they grant to the question of the body is a central point of their works. The movements of the 1960s and 1970s—a founding experience for many of them—were an arena of discovery of collective action in which, beyond the utopian imagination and the critique of domination, sexual liberation was theorized and practiced. The social fabrication of gender is inscribed in the body, as are certain more individual and intimate existential turns. Steedman's life stories explain, among other things, her own refusal of biological motherhood. Passerini gives several examples of her way of somatizing certain affects; when her father dies, she is seized by a feeling of guilt— the fear of not having been a good daughter—which leads her to the edge of the "abyss": "I felt a bundle of muscles between my stomach and abdomen relax and contract. Spasms, shaking, and sobs."[28] With age, she also becomes aware of her resemblance to her mother: "Every day I discover new sides of my mother: I remember her slender but strong hips, the solidity of the abdomen that carried me and to which I can entrust myself, I feel that she cared about me, I rediscover the security of being loved."[29] She believes that she is able to "speak to her inner image which I carry within myself."[30] Recalling with Joan Wallach

Scott that the very notion of "women" is a cultural construct, Passerini does not make the female body the sign of destiny; rather, she sees it as a sort of interface, a place of interaction between the biological and the cultural, between the material and symbolic dimensions of a life. This experience of the body being shared explains a certain feminist reluctance to say "I," a pronoun more often replaced, as in the case of Wallach Scott, by an "ego-historical plural" in which the "we" sometimes designates female historians and feminists and sometimes women.[31]

■ ■ ■

Of course, the typology I have established is not exhaustive. Its selective character is due, among other things, to the limits of my linguistic knowledge and fields of competence, but it brings together the most well-known figures and constitutes a significant sample all the same. The "geopolitical" dimension of these historian autobiographies is not without interest. The vast majority of them come from the Anglo-American world and, to a lesser extent, from France. Among them we find a considerable number of Jewish authors, a collection of fractured lives and unconventional pathways, and, as a result, a powerful desire to save the legacy of a submerged world. On the other hand, these life stories bring out a characteristic feature of Western culture at the start of the twenty-first century: when an autobiographical story sets out to account for an intellectual journey and to place its existential dimension in a historical context, especially that of the interwar period, it is the author's status as "victim" (or as close to victims) that seems to give it legitimacy. It is striking to note that, compared to the considerable number of memoirs of exiles, there are few autobiographies of historians who have experienced fascist regimes *in situ.* The autobiographies of German Jewish exiles far exceed those of their colleagues in the Federal Republic, who nevertheless constitute an incomparably larger cohort. The era when Friedrich Meinecke wrote his memoirs as a sort of academic *Bildungsroman* is over.[32] Today, the autobiographies of German historians are exceptions (like that of Nicolaus Sombart) or bear witness to other unsettled lives,[33] such as those of "survivors" of the Democratic Republic of Germany (for example, Jürgen Kuczynski and Hans Mayer, who, however, were also exiled Jews).[34] In Italy and Spain, autobiographies of historians are almost nonexistent, even among those who had to flee fascism (Gaetano Salvemini is an exception).[35] This is a shame, because the transition of Delio Cantimori from fascism to communism, the exile and antifascist choice of Arnaldo Momigliano, the expatriation of Juan-José Carreras, or the training in Francoist Spain of a Marxist historian such as Josep Fontana would undoubtedly have given rise to fascinating stories.[36]

While these "transgressions" remain isolated moments in a historian's itinerary, recognition of the subjective dimension implicit in historical research, of the fact that historians inject a part of themselves into their works, has been far more frequent in the past twenty years. This admission that once seemed almost obscene, like the violation of a taboo or the confession of sin, has gradually been accepted as a form of intellectual honesty. Thus, at the start of his *The Age of Extremes* (1994), Eric J.

Hobsbawm remembers having lived the twentieth century as an adult: "My own lifetime coincides with most of the period with which this book deals, and for most of it, from early teenage to the present, I have been conscious in public affairs, that is to say I have accumulated views and prejudices about it as a contemporary rather than as a scholar."[37] As a historian, he specifies, his "period" is the nineteenth century, and therefore his book is ultimately a departure from his disciplinary choices. In short, the reader should know that he wrote his work as a "committed spectator" as much as a historian: "No one who has lived through this extraordinary century is likely to abstain from judgement. It is understanding that comes hard."[38]

In his preface to *The Passing of an Illusion* (1995), François Furet admits the "biographical connection" in the theme of his book. "My subject is thus inseparable from my existence," he writes, adding that he intensely experienced the "illusion" whose course he traces in order to analyze it.[39] Four decades after his break with the Communist Party, he thus reconsiders his "erstwhile blindness with neither indulgence nor acrimony." Without indulgence, because his aim is anything but apologetic— his book will be the culmination of a vast anticommunist campaign after the fall of the USSR—and without acrimony, because he was able to learn the lessons of that "unfortunate engagement" of his youth.

Paul Fussell, author of *The Great War and Modern Memory* (1975), a work that introduced cultural history into military studies, underscores the extent to which his own experience as an American soldier wounded in the south of France during World War II allowed him to explore the corporeal dimension of modern warfare.[40] Omer Bartov, to whom we owe a reference work on the German soldiers mobilized on the Eastern Front between 1941 and 1945, admits to having also forged an "empathetic" connection with the subjects of his study. "My personal experiences as an Israeli soldier and citizen," he writes in the preface to *Hitler's Army: Soldiers, Nazis, and War in the Third Reich* (1991), "have had a substantial, if indirect impact on my views as a historian. When writing about the Wehrmacht I found myself drawing on my own experiences."[41] This helped him understand the mental world of the German military, although he obviously could not identify with the purpose of their war.

From the observation of the subjectivity inherent in their works, some historians have tried to integrate it as a legitimate, not to mention necessary, dimension of their methodology. One can easily perceive the traces, in this effort, of the influence of psychoanalysis, which enabled historians to become aware of the moments of "transfer" that intervene in their approach to the past. In his introduction to the second volume of *Nazi Germany and the Jews* (2007), Saul Friedländer emphasizes that the historicization of National Socialism must give way to the memory of victims, which requires the intervention of the subjectivity of the historians themselves. Conducting their investigation, the latter tend to construct a "protective shield" that separates them from their object, thus establishing the distance that is the very premise of historical knowledge. However, it happens this screen is suddenly torn by the discovery of a source—a document, a letter, an image, any material object, including the most banal—that arouses an intense emotion, generates in them a strong empathetic identification, and thus throws disorder into their tidy workshop. This kind of "transfer" is both an epistemological obstacle and an advantage for historians working on the twentieth century. If they manage to master and surmount it, the emotional turmoil can prove fruitful, especially if they work with experiences filed in administrative archives that tend to reify, fix, and "freeze" the past.

According to Friedländer, the emergence of an "individual voice" can "tear the seamless interpretation" and call scholarly "detachment" and "objectivity" into question. This "disruptive function," which endangers the linearity of the narrative, he believes, can become "essential to the historical representation of mass extermination and other sequences of mass suffering that 'business as usual historiography' necessarily domesticates and 'flattens.'"[42] Mobilizing the psychoanalytic lexicon, Friedländer defines the search for a balance between distancing and empathic identification as a process of "working through" (Freudian *Durcharbeitung*),[43] which makes it possible to avoid the impasses—contradictory but convergent—where the emotional surge leads like cold and soothing reification, memorial fetishism like the naivety of linear narratives.

The emergence of the "I" narrative in contemporary historiography might be seen, in several respects, as a response to this methodological questioning. A response from a generation that, unlike Hobsbawm, Furet, or Friedländer, did not live through the time it was studying and should therefore make no effort to keep it at a distance. The part of subjectivity it injects into the narrative of the past becomes a modality of interpretation; it is no longer the result of a confrontation between lived experience and knowledge, even less of the working through of a trauma suffered.

Chapter Four

SHORT INVENTORY OF "I" NARRATIVES

BUT WHAT happens if, instead of being a stage that the historian manages to master and fruitfully enter into research, the "transfer" referred to by Friedländer becomes the very matrix of his writing of the past? What if the historian makes this intimate turmoil an engine of both his investigation and his narration? Over the past decade, we have witnessed the birth of a new kind of historical narrative that, without being autobiographical in the conventional sense of the word, involves a total symbiosis between the historian and his object of investigation. Its privileged place remains France, but it quickly made its appearance in other countries, even if its scale is not yet easy to measure. This new narrative is based primarily on the parental legacy or the genealogy of its authors and takes the form of a family story that seeks to shed light on the history of a society as a whole.

The author is one of the protagonists of the story. I will give here some of the best-known examples.

■ ■ ■

State sociologist and internationally known historian of "State Jews" and anti-Semitism in France, Pierre Birnbaum had never, in his numerous works, mentioned his past as a hidden child. Born in Lourdes in July of 1940, a few weeks after the defeat and the exodus, to Jewish parents who immigrated to France in 1933, he survived, during the war, hidden by a family of peasants from Omex, a village in the High Pyrenees, near Lourdes. For a long time, he kept this past at a distance, thinking it should not interfere with his work as a scholar. It was only at the insistence of a close friend of the Hebrew University of Jerusalem that he agreed, in the 1990s, to be interviewed by Deborah Dwork, a Yale professor who was collecting testimonies about the hidden children of the Holocaust. Until then, he had felt a certain reluctance to "speak as an object of History, far from [his] posture as a scholar anxious to rule out, as our teacher Émile Durkheim would say, all preconceptions, values, any form of subjectivity."[1] It was only much later, in 2018, that he decided to become a historian of himself; not a "witness," because he did not want to make a "literary account" of his life, but a rigorous scholar and analyst of his own past.[2] Hence the subtitle of his book, "a personal history," and the detailed documentation—collected in the archives of the High Pyrenees—on the hunt for Jewish people and, more precisely, his own family, that structures it.

The book is full of affection for Marie and Fabien, the two farmers who saved him, thus deserving the posthumous status of Righteous Among the Nations, but presents itself as the story of the persecution of a Jewish family during the war. To tell the truth, this account takes place primarily in the first part of the work, which, subsequently, turns into an essay of historical self-analysis where Pierre Birnbaum retraces the stages of his awareness of the anti-Semitism of Vichy. Filled with republican convictions and enshrined in a long tradition of "State Jews" who give everything to their country, he had long lived in denial of state anti-Semitism.[3] In 1981, he did not want to read the book by Michael Marrus and Robert O. Paxton that revealed and analyzed the completely French character of the anti-Semitic laws promulgated by the Vichy regime in October of 1940. Then, little by little, he faced the facts.[4] He did not question the cult he devoted to the state—"it is therefore not the state that betrays the Jews, it is a de facto power that has become legal if not legitimate," embodied by servile senior officials—but he had to recognize that Vichy was a "pathological moment" for this same state.[5] Under German occupation, the French state persecuted the Jews; it was above all peasants, representatives of a rural France perceived as backward, who saved them, along with ecclesiastics and Protestants. This problematization of his republican convictions caused a major methodological change in his path as a historian, and he was subsequently able to write as a scholar in the first person.

La leçon de Vichy is only the most recent in a long list of works on subjectivist history. In *Composition française* (2009), famous historian of the French Revolution Mona Ozouf describes her childhood divided between the almost exclusively Breton identity of her family, the universalist and national-republican education received at school, and the conservatism of the Catholic Church: these three pillars of modern France have marked her life and forged her personality. The tension between these different elements could be strong, sometimes violent, but she knew how to manage it: "Brittany lived at home in the person of my grandmother, and yet it was she who spoke to me about France. The France taught at school was the one that the house designated as our hereditary enemy, stubbornly unifying and centralizing, and yet it was also the country which had made, in pedagogically ordered sequences, a march towards justice and democracy, in which way it was a rational homeland more than an empirical homeland, and, to this the house could subscribe without betraying its Breton faith."[6] Her first-person narrative takes on a paradigmatic character that goes beyond her individual journey to become the key to interpreting a larger, national history.

In *Jeanne et les siens* (2003), Michel Winock, historian of the Third Republic and of intellectuals, likewise retraces the history of his family.[7] He does so as a historian, consulting departmental archives both in the North, where the family of his father Gaston, a transport worker of Flemish origin, is from, and in the Paris region, where his mother Jeanne, who ran a grocery store in Arcueil, is from. As her father died at the end of the war, Jeanne held a prominent place alongside her brothers: Marcel, who died of tuberculosis during the Liberation, and Pierre, who helped young Michel with his studies. Once again, beyond this mosaic of portraits filled with affection, a piece of

French history is contained in the fate of this family, with the illustration of the relationship of the popular classes to culture, religion, and politics.

Quelle histoire: Un récit de filiation (2013) by Stéphane Audoin-Rouzeau is another family story that begins with the Great War and ends with his choice to become a historian of war. A story, if you will, of a homecoming. Three of his grandparents were mobilized and returned from the trenches. Robert, his paternal grandfather, was a nationalist who sacrificed his "best years" at the front, which led to the radical antimilitarism of his son, Philippe, revolutionary and member of the Surrealist movement, and father of the author. Stéphane therefore assumes his vocation as a historian as a sort of "subtle betrayal" of his father's commitments to the radical left and loyalty to his grandparents. He retraces this itinerary through an investigation carried out by applying his "research protocols" to the adventures of his family. Beyond a simple biography, his book is intended to be an investigation well anchored in the "field of history."[8]

In *Un fantôme dans la bibliothèque* (2017), a collection of writings filled with memories, written at different times, Maurice Olender describes how the child that he was, coming from "a world of orality where one endlessly discussed what no longer existed," a child who fiercely refused to learn to read and write, to the great despair of his father, became the scholar we know, a comparative historian of languages and religions. Conscious of the multiple springs of archival accumulation—including a desire to forget, since sometimes "we archive above all in order to have the right to a deep sleep"[9]—he spent his life saving everything, including train tickets for his regular trips between Paris and Brussels. His book illustrates the intimate link that unites his existential trajectory and his choices as a historian.

The most significant example of this new form of family history, however, remains *A History of the Grandparents I Never Had* by Ivan Jablonka (2012), one of the greatest commercial successes ever achieved by a history book published in France within the last decades. As the title suggests, this is an investigation into the lives of his grandparents, Matès and Idesa Jablonka, both Polish Jews who emigrated to France before being deported and killed at Auschwitz. The book begins with these words: "I have set out, as a historian, in search of the grandparents I never had. Because their lives were over long before mine began, Matès and Idesa Jablonka are at once close relatives and perfect strangers. They were faceless victims of the great twentieth-century tragedies: Stalinism, World War II, and the annihilation of European Jewry."[10]

Jablonka thus wrote this work, as he points out in the incipit, "as a historian," and he admirably reconstructed the lives of his grandparents by mobilizing the tools and methodologies of historical research. His book has been published in history collections both in France and the United States. However, it would be extremely reductive to qualify it simply as a work of history, since its historical tableau is completely imbued with the affects of the author and his *pietas*, in the original sense of the term: a feeling of devotion that leads to fulfilling duties with regard to his parents (or grandparents). "You can be sure that when you are dead, I'll be thinking of you sadly for the rest of my life. Even when my life is over for me too, my own children know about you. And even their children will know about you when I am in my grave. For me, you'll be my gods, my beloved gods who will watch over me and nobody else. I will be thinking: my gods are my shield, whether I am in heaven or hell."[11] This lyrical style is that of a letter Jablonka wrote to his grandparents as a child. He made it the premise of his book, which is not common for the pen of a historian.

Jablonka adopted the same method for two other inquiries. The first, *Laëtitia* (2016), moved thousands of readers.[12] It focuses upon a news item, a homicide that made headlines and aroused strong emotions, even becoming a state affair when it was exploited by President Nicolas Sarkozy for political reasons. In his book, the historian reconstructs the murder and tells the life of the victim, an eighteen-year-old young woman, Laëtitia Perrais, who was placed in a foster family with her twin sister, Jessica, following the violence inflicted upon them by their alcoholic father. A waitress in a restaurant in the suburbs of Nantes, Perrais was killed in 2011 by a sexual attacker. This story, which Jablonka presents as a "criminal investigation" and at the same time a "life investigation,"[13] has a double objective: on the one hand, to show what a heinous crime perpetrated in a suburban area may reveal about the desolation of our societies, the condition of childhood and of youth in a poor and abandoned environment; on the other hand, to portray a young woman, describing her difficulties, experiences, hopes, and dreams, bringing her out of anonymity to give her back her life. "I would like to show," writes Jablonka, "that a news item (*fait divers*) can be analyzed as an object of history."[14] His latest book, *En camping-car* (2018), a much lighter account of his childhood vacations, also aims to develop a family memoir and to describe the summer holidays of the middle classes in the 1980s. Once again, a family chronicle written in the first person and general history intersect until they become inseparable: "A historian of childhood, I wanted to evoke mine as a historian. As a social science writer, I wanted to turn this discipline towards me, turn it against me, present myself to it."[15]

The subjectivity of history actors—not those who act in the foreground, upon whom the spotlight shines, but the anonymous, the neglected, the forgotten of ordinary life, those who have been marginalized—is at the heart of the works of Philippe Artières, one of the most creative and original historians of the last two decades. In Michel Foucault's wake, he looked at the "guilty lives," stigmatized and condemned, of a multitude of murderers, parricides, prostitutes, thieves, and ruffians, thus removing them from the grip of criminal anthropology, where they had been relegated since the end of the nineteenth century.[16] Contrary to approaches that, since the medical and social sciences of the time, try to explain mental illness and unravel the secret of crime, Artières decided to "walk" with their violent and abused lives, to "accompany" them so as to allow us to hear their voices. Suddenly, their stories emancipated them from the subaltern places from which they were engendered and became "processes of subjectivation," in the Foucauldian sense of the term, where the historian acted as the "border-crosser." It is by following the same method, and with the collaboration of Dominique Kalifa, that Artières reconstructed the life of Henri Vidal, the "killer of women" who made headlines in 1901, by composing the "autobiography" of the murderer himself, based on the articles the press had devoted to him and the testimonies left by the many actors of his judicial incidents (police officers, magistrates, doctors, etc.).[17] Through this complex montage operation that articulates and composes archival material as a filmmaker edits the images of his film, Artières and Kalifa questioned the conventional methods of writing history and tried to invent, from its raw materials, a new story of the past.

In his latest works, *Vie et mort de Paul Gény* (2013) and *Au fond* (2016), both published in a literary collection, Artières applied his historiographical method to the investigation of his own history and that of his family, of which he became the narrator.[18] Paul Gény, a Jesuit father and professor of philosophy at the Gregorian University, assassinated in Rome in October 1925 by a soldier who stuck his bayonet in his back, was his great-uncle. During a one-year stay at the Villa Medici, Artières sketched a portrait of the victim, reconstructed the murder, and found in the city archives the traces of his murderer, a man named Bambino Marchi who, declared insane, did not undergo any trial, but spent the rest of his life in a psychiatric hospital. So it was Bambino's life even more than Paul's that attracted the historian, to the point that he reproduced the archives: its fragmentary texts, photos, and press clippings.

In *Au fond*, Artières looks back on a painful story that grieved his family, the sudden death of his brother at the age of three, before his own birth, and that his mother told him about fifty years later, thus ending her mourning. The author travels to the scene of the tragedy, a small town in Moselle, Saint-Avold, where his parents lived at the time, in an area he discovers while describing it. His father worked there as a manager in the disappearing mining industry. The historian finds the archives of the miners' strikes, the documents attesting to the accidents at work in which many of them lost their lives, and the struggles of their wives who went to Paris to defend their rights and make their voices heard without being received at the Élysée by de Gaulle.

Constructed like the author's previous works, with archival material reproduced in the framework of the book and identifiable through typographical variations, *Vie et mort de Paul Gény* and *Au fond* are, above all, investigative accounts. At times playful, painful, emotional, and enriching, they are always, in the final analysis, an investigation and a writing of the self. In *Vie et mort de Paul Gény*, the author borrows several heteronyms: he describes his stay at the Villa Medici and his Roman investigations into the murder of his great-uncle in the first person; then he dons the clothes of the murderer's brother to affectionately address him in recounting his life;[19] finally, in the last part of the book, he returns to his investigation by staging himself, in the third person, as a researcher who travels between Paris, Trieste, and Reggio Emilia to participate in conferences and to show the affinities between his Foucauldian works and Franco Basaglia's antipsychiatry.

Paul Gény, the ancestor whose assassination sparked this whole investigation, turns out to be almost a mere pretext. Artières pays homage to him by bringing back several archival items, including a letter and an article written by one of his Jesuit colleagues; he also has a commemorative plaque put up in the street where the crime was perpetrated, San Basilio, with an inscription from the time, the rhetoric of which now seems very outdated. The work of the Jesuit great-uncle—a man who, by all accounts, "passionately loved philosophy as science and apostolate"; a man who, "for philosophy, said that he had left everything: literature, art, all other relief for the mind"—does not interest Artières.[20] "The whole thing is very boring," he writes of his books, mentioning a treaty on the theory of knowledge, error, and syllogism, and honestly acknowledging that he feels "a stranger to this world."[21] He neither cites nor mentions any title of Gény's works. On the other hand, in the name of a playful and aesthetic practice of historiography, he buys a cassock at Barbiconi on Santa Caterina, the shop that dresses Roman ecclesiastics, and begins to walk in the streets of the city disguised as a priest. With the complicity of two friends, he even makes a reconstruction of the murder, the "photo-history" of which would become the subject of a later work.[22] He admits, in an interview for *La vie des idées*, that this restitution can "make people smile or appear as a narcissistic practice."[23] Indeed, the *in situ* performance has little to do with the memory of a "relived" experience that Claude Lanzmann tried to elicit among the witnesses interviewed in *Shoah*.

Artières conceives of history as an exploration involving a corporeal, physical relationship of the scholar with the material of the past, but he did not have his back pierced by a bayonet and he would not accept, one imagines, going to Auschwitz wearing striped pajamas or a SS uniform. This playful desire for reincarnation carries risks, first of all that of confusing research practices with the performances of the artist or, worse, with the amused curiosity of the tourist. Published in a hybrid collection, his book plays with the mixture of genres with virtuosity, but this does not fail to arouse, beyond a smile, a certain discomfort among historians.

Unlike his victim, the murderer, Bambino Marchi, is portrayed in a more vivid and nuanced manner. A traumatized soldier of the Great War, he kills to avenge his mother who committed suicide after a priest made her believe that her son had died in combat. Perhaps this is why, in dressing in his brother's clothes, the author uses the *tu* form with him out of empathy, which he fails to do with his great-uncle. It is when speaking of Bambino that, at the conclusion of his book, he refers to the anonymous one who became his brother, "the one who helps me to walk, to go all the way."[24] The hypotheses he formulates on how, at the time, "the history of madness never ceased to cross social and political history" are interesting, and he is right to underscore that "Bambino and Paul were not protagonists of a news item, but of a history of the twentieth century."[25] These assumptions, however, are barely stated. There is nothing in the book about Bambino's war experience or the postwar violence he undoubtedly witnessed and from which fascism arose. If, as Laurent Demanze rightly points out, Artières uses the archive as "plastic material" or as a "piece to exhibit,"[26] in these two books he makes it the source of a largely decontextualized literary narrative that does not aim to produce knowledge, but only to stage an investigation in which the real hero is the author himself. The result is a seductive and literary work, but one that only summons the past to generate the narrative of the questions and emotions it arouses in the narrator.[27]

Another example of autobiographical history, all the more interesting in that it moves away, this time from family sagas, investigations into missing relatives, and war stories, is *La traversée des Alpes* (2014) by Antoine de Baecque.[28] A well-known historian of the French Revolution, the body, and especially cinema, de Baecque has been a passionate hiker since his adolescence. His book is simultaneously a scholarly work and an autobiographical account. A scholarly work, because it focuses on the history of the GR5, official name since 1950 of the path that connects Lake Geneva to the Mediterranean, and a travel narrative, since it relates how de Baecque traveled it himself in September of 2009, with a thirty-seven-pound backpack on his shoulders, walking from Saint-Gingolph to Nice. The two parallel narratives, to tell the truth, are enticing. The historiographical essay on the GR5 is at the intersection of religious history (medieval pilgrimages), economic history (fabric exchanges and transhumance), political and military history (the establishment of borders, the construction of fortresses), history of mobility (from population transfer to the illegal trafficking of smugglers), history of the environment (how, over the centuries, people have marked out, traversed, plowed, and modeled the land, shaping its landscape), history of bodies (how mountains shape the bodies of those who inhabit them or test those of walkers), and also, more recently, the history of tourism, which has unearthed trails threatened by abandonment and has now become the main economic resource of this region at the crossroads of France, Switzerland, and Italy. Starting from a striking analogy between the historian and the walker—"[the]

historian accumulates, compares, interprets strata of historical materials exactly like the walker acquires and reconstructs a vision-experience of the surrounding world along the way"[29]— and of the observation that the path traveled has "a plural temporal depth" that has metamorphosed the walker into an "object of history," de Baecque makes his walk into an archive. His book therefore brings together the history of a mountain and a travel diary that meticulously details the stages of his journey, sometimes a source of ecstasy and sometimes an ordeal.

Only writing, he explains, "could weave together the private diary of a lived walk and its historical reflexivity."[30] The text, however, has two different, parallel writing levels, well separated in the book not only by chapters that alternate general history and first-person narrative but also by distinct typefaces. Yet the travel diary has nothing of the historiographical essay and all of the literary autobiography, because it speaks to us of the fears and the excitement of the author before the departure, of his professional concerns—he organizes his hike during a period of unemployment—and his hesitation to leave his daughters and his pregnant wife in Paris; nor does he spare us the smallest details about the state of his body before, during, and after this ordeal: the pain in the feet, inflammation, and deformed toenails: "I have horn claws instead of toenails that frighten all who see them. A podiatrist consulted before the hike told me there was nothing more to do." He inherited his toenails from his father: "When he removed his shoes and socks it was a horror. When I take my socks off, it is yet another horror."[31] Sometimes the pleasure of the narrative takes on a fictional character, when, for example, at the start of his trip, he thinks of his arrival in Nice and is obsessed with the fantasy of "having sex with a Russian whore at the Negresco."[32] When he arrives, however, he looks like "a vagrant, at least a backpacker, lost, marginal, lousy and smelly, since it is obviously incongruous for a passer-by of the avenue Jean-Médecin to think that [he] has come straight from crossing the Alps."[33] This crossing of the Alps is therefore also a crossing of genres in which history meets literature, and the impersonal account of historical reconstruction the narrative "I" of autobiography. Needless to add that, a few years ago, a historical collection—in this case Gallimard's "Library of Histories"—would not have welcomed a work constructed like a private diary. A history of crossing the Alps, even on foot, did not need a confession full of details about toenails, aching feet, insect bites, and the erotic fantasies of the walker. If the author felt the need to share these details, it is because his text also wanted to be something else, a diary, precisely, and meet an additional criterion, that of autobiographical writing.

Another example of historical writing in which the autobiographical dimension is omnipresent, *Primo Levi's Resistance* (2016) by Sergio Luzzatto, reconstructs and interprets the ephemeral experience of Primo Levi in the ranks of the Resistance, just before his arrest and deportation to Auschwitz. The "trace," in this case, is an enigmatic passage from the *The Periodic Table* (1975), an autobiographical and literary text that takes the form of a chemistry textbook. In this allusive, but deliberately vague, passage, Levi recalls the devastating experience of the execution of two "traitors" within his small group of partisans: "We had been forced by our conscience to carry out a sentence, and we had done so, but we had emerged destroyed, destitute, desiring that everything be finished and to be finished ourselves; but desiring also to see each other, to talk, to help one another exorcise that still so recent memory."[34] Based on this fragile evidence, Luzzatto succeeds in reconstructing the history of this group of young, inexperienced Resistance fighters, its composition, its networks, and its amateurism. On the military level, it was not until after Levi's arrest by the fascist police in December of 1943 that the Resistance flourished.[35] Between the armistice of September 8, 1943, and the end of the year, the Italian Resistance began to organize in the mountains and still struggled to define its political profile and distinguish itself from banditry; this work involved the establishment of very strict, sometimes brutal rules.[36] Luzzatto identified the two executed youths and elucidated the facts behind their convictions. Their execution disguised as death in combat and their transformation from "traitors" to martyrs reveal behind the scenes of the Resistance, as much heroic as cruel, often idealized and simplified. Before his deportation, Levi therefore experienced another tragic dimension of World War II, that of partisans who execute traitors among their comrades. Luzzatto's book brings an important new element to both Levi's biography and the history of the Resistance. It is another microhistory that sheds light upon a much larger landscape.

What makes this book a captivating tale, however, is its narrative style: the portrayal of the witnesses interviewed, the description of their encounters, and the splendid storyline of the partisan struggle. He describes his excursions into the mountains, which were the backdrop for the fighters, the breathtaking landscapes laid out before their eyes and the morphology of the Alps that gave the partisan struggle its telluric character. He does not hide his scruples in the face of these old fighters and witnesses whose stories awaken in him childhood memories— the stories his parents told him about the Resistance—and he shares his emotions with the reader. The description of his meeting with Aldo Piacenza, an old Piedmontese partisan, in his house, is gripping:

> When I was taken in to see Piacenza in his studio overlooking the gardens outside, he had his back to the door. He was facing the window, with a blanket over his knees. Waiting for me, it seemed, and perhaps for something more. I was touched by the sight of him, in part because it made me think of the wheelchair used for so long by my mother; in part because the man before me was the very image of the stalwart old partisan. For a second, I felt like a character from the period I had studied for my thesis many years before, like one of the French Republicans who during the 1820s and '30s—battling the enemies of the Revolution—would go to visit the old Montagnards, the last Jacobin survivors of 1793, and collect their memories as a sign of gratitude. Seated there beside Aldo Piacenza, I was briefly a son who had recently lost the mother who once read him the last letters of partisans condemned to death—and a citizen infinitely grateful to an old man like Piacenza for having been a partisan in the hills in his youth, for having made Italy free. More than a few moments went by before I regained the more neutral guise of the historian.[37]

Mark Mazower's *What You Did Not Tell: A Russian Past and the Journey Home* (2017) is a good example of family history published in the English-speaking world.[38] The book recounts the journey of two generations, again focusing on the author's paternal grandparents: Max, who was first a member of the Bund—a Jewish, socialist, and anti-Zionist political movement—under the Tsarist regime and in interwar Poland, before becoming a successful businessman in London; and Frouma, his wife, who had survived the Terror in Stalin's Russia. Central and Eastern Europe, Vilnius, Stalingrad, occupied Paris during the war, and finally London, where Mark was born and raised: these are the settings, cities, geographical backdrop, historical and existential framework in which the lives of his grandparents intersect, whom he has endeavored to restore through a large number of sources drawn from his family's archives, from identity papers to letters and photographs. Like Jablonka's books, Mazower's is an intimate account that provides insight into the history of European Jews in the twentieth century.

Another example, Omer Bartov's book *Anatomy of a Genocide: The Life and Death of a Town Called Buczacz* (2018), however, is not written in the first person. It recounts the Holocaust through the prism of a small town in Central Europe, now located in Ukraine, after having belonged to the Hapsburg Empire and to Poland. A peaceful location where Ukrainians, Poles, and Jews had lived together for centuries, which suddenly became, during the war, a theater of terror and extreme violence. Buczacz was also the hometown of the author's mother, who recalls her childhood in the first pages of the book. The idea of writing this work came to him specifically from their conversations in the family home in Tel Aviv. *Anatomy of a Genocide* is a work of microhistory—a small window that opens onto a larger landscape—the result of two decades of research in multiple countries and archives, but its backdrop nevertheless remains very personal, and its author does not hide the halo of memories and feelings that envelops him. This book, Bartov writes, "was nourished by a network of support and wisdom, institutional and professional, as well as personal and emotional, so thick and dense and entirely indispensable that I would never be able to sufficiently thank and acknowledge it." This business, he adds, "seemed to have taken on a life of its own and to have entirely taken over mine."[39]

NARRATIVIZING THE INVESTIGATION

The staging of the inquiry constitutes a major methodological change specific to this new writing of history rooted in the intimacy of the author, but that proposes to interpret the past of an entire society or to analyze a historical experience as a whole. The authors of these works reveal their doubts and hesitations, describe their encounters with witnesses and their immersion in the archives, the enthusiasm and disappointment aroused by their discoveries, as well as their emotions at a story taking shape before their eyes. The inquiry is no longer just the premise of their story, the means of accessing and exploiting a source, the underground work that creates and plows the material of which a story is made; the investigation becomes an integral part of the story itself. In *Au fond*, Philippe Artières describes his arrival at the Departmental Archives of Saint-Julien-lès-Metz, in Moselle, in October 2014:

> I have just received my card and my reader number without which I cannot access any documents; I took the bus by the station and got off at the end of the line; I finally sit down in the reading room; we are three; a very agitated man speaks loudly, he has just located the birthdate of his great-grandfather. Finding traces of ancestors in the Archives is easy, but searching for a buried memory can take years. I do surveys, I note call numbers, I order files; I try to figure out what life was like in a mining town like the one my parents lived in early in the 1960s.[40]

And here is a passage, among others like it, drawn from *A History of the Grandparents I Never Had*, which constitutes a significant example of this storytelling as an account of historical inquiry. Jablonka discovers that the national security forces file listing foreigners inspected for their political activities, which includes his grandparents, was brought back to France after being confiscated by the Germans in 1940, then seized by the Soviets in 1945, and finally returned in the early 1990s. He therefore rushes to consult it:

> So here I am: armed with my laptop and my digital camera, I hop on an early train from the Gare de Lyon, ready to dig into the National Security files. The indexing system is distributed among thousands of cardboard boxes, each containing

hundreds of individual cards, and each card refers you to that person's complete file made up of reports, memos, forms, ID photos, correspondence between the person in question and the police, the ministry and various associations, all this paperwork suddenly ushering me into the private, desperate world of people now deceased.[41]

The "evidential paradigm" at the origin of the survey is no longer hidden; on the contrary, it is permanently exhibited. In a famous essay, Carlo Ginzburg discerned this epistemological model—based on deductions and cross-referencing drawn from "clues"—in Freud's dream interpretations, the expertise of the art critic Giovanni Morelli, and the detective novels of Arthur Conan Doyle.[42] This paradigm, he suggested, became an essential device of the social sciences at the end of the nineteenth century, which explains its appropriation by historical research. It is exactly this analytical device that new historiography exposes to make it a key element of its narration. The "detective," who reconstructs the events, analyzes their links, suggests or evaluates the motives of the actors, and exhibits the evidence, no longer hides behind an anonymous narrative in the third person. It shows itself on every page. Stressing that the report of the investigation makes it possible to grasp the grain of a historical tableau, Jablonka rejects the "aesthetics of the finished product," which he sees as the equivalent, in the social sciences, of academicism in art history.[43] Of course, this narrativization of the investigation does not erase the boundaries that separate history from fiction, since it accompanies and nurtures a historical narrative that must be "incontrovertible" and "based on evidence," resisting "the lure of pure imagination."[44] The fact remains that the participation of the historian as a narrator in the story recounted breaks the conventional forms of historical discourse, invites the reader into the workshop, and confers on the text a simultaneously self-reflexive and fictional quality.[45]

SOCIOLOGICAL INTERMEZZO

A small parenthesis should be opened here, as the narrative "I" has entered another domain that, until recently, was hermetically closed to it. After historians, sociologists also began to write in the first person in their autobiographies as well as in their studies, even in autobiographies that take the form of an investigation. The phenomenon is new, because sociology has always been the temple of objectivity. Max Weber and Émile Durkheim, founders of the discipline, were categorical on this point. The former refused to bring together social sciences and art. In his eyes, with knowledge having an objective character and being submitted to the laws of cumulative progress, obsolescence was the inevitable fate of scientific works. Art, on the other hand, seemed eminently subjective and timeless to him. He recognized, of course, that works of art are born in a given historical context of which they bear traces, but their historicity, he explained, does not condemn them to desuetude. We admire the statues of antiquity and the painting of the Middle Ages, which continue to inspire awe and arouse emotions within us. Their uniqueness stems from the subjectivity of their creators, but their communicative power is not eroded or diminished by time. Art—like eroticism in another human sphere—escapes the unforgiving constraints of scientific rationality.[46] The production of knowledge, on the other hand, presupposes going beyond or sublimating the "ego" of scholars; knowledge is objective and "axiologically neutral" (*wertfrei*).

Durkheim, for his part, became famous for explaining that, in order to understand suicide, it was above all necessary to disregard its subjective motivations. It should not be viewed as the extreme and tragic culmination of an existential crisis, as a choice linked to the suffering, fatigue, or unhappiness of human beings. He stressed that it was necessary to approach it as a social fact with regularity and variations that we may study. Durkheim is the heir of early positivism considering literature as a form of metaphysical knowledge doomed to disappear with the triumph of scientific mind. To be recognized as a discipline in its own right, sociology had to be distinguished from literature, the domain of imagination and subjectivity. In *Between Literature and Science* (1988), Wolf Lepenies showed the extent to which, in France, England, and Germany at the turn of the twentieth century, this shock was violent. For conservative thought, the advent of sociology represented a cultural catastrophe and a threat to classical culture.[47] When it comes to sociologists, they could certainly be interested in literature, but they had to do so keeping a certain distance, carefully avoiding the slightest mix of genres. Even at the end of the 1980s, Jean-Claude Passeron recalled what seemed obvious to him: "We have often seen good literature made with bad sociology, sometimes even with good, never good sociology with literature, good or bad."[48] Consequently, just as with historians, the autobiographies of sociologists were inevitably transgressions permitted by the notoriety of their authors.

Equally powerful was anthropology's repugnance toward subjectivity. According to Claude Lévi-Strauss, history, which worked with documents from actors of the past, was the science of change, while anthropology, which was interested in structures, required an external perspective, that of a scholar "foreign" to the group studied.[49] Structuralism, he wrote, was thus to "disregard the subject," a disturbing element that he saw as an "unbearably spoilt child who has occupied the philosophical scene for too long now, and prevented serious research through demanding exclusive attention."[50]

The first genuine autobiography written by a sociologist was published nearly a century after the birth of this discipline and has a remarkable literary dimension. Richard Hoggart's *A Local Habitation* (1988) is a very personal, intimate text, which describes the upward social journey of an orphan from a working-class district of Leeds, son of a construction worker, who first became a professor of literature at the University of Birmingham, where he founded the school of cultural studies with Stuart Hall, then of sociology at the University of London. In this work, the author applies the tools of sociological analysis upon himself to study his deep cultural and emotional attachment to his home environment, in which he experiences "an intense feeling of quiet happiness and assurance."[51] This book has become a model of autobiographical writing and has shaken, as one can easily imagine, the standards of its discipline: subjectivity and literature made their way into sociology.

This precedent undoubtedly made the task easier for Pierre Bourdieu, even if his *Sketch for a Self-Analysis* (2008) has no literary pretensions and limits itself to applying the rules of sociological research to his own life and scholarly trajectory, thus explaining how his habitus took shape.[52] To do this, he talks about his Bearn childhood in a modest family, his boarding school education, his Algerian experience, then his accession to the École Normale Supérieure, his readings and his teachers. Encouraged, no doubt, by this first pioneering essay, other sociologists felt the need to write about themselves, not only to reflect on their intellectual trajectory but to speak about their life, families, experiences, and self.

One of the most beautiful books born from this transgression of the "rules of the sociological method" is *Returning to Reims* by Didier Eribon (2009), disciple of Bourdieu. The first return to a "region of myself," to use the expression he borrows from Jean Genet, this essay starts from an essential premise.[53] After many years devoted to the study of forms of gay sexual subjectivation through a method inspired by Foucault and Bourdieu, Eribon came to the following conclusion: his career as a sociologist was spurred by a desire to flee his original milieu, the social world that was his own, that of the working class of a provincial town, Reims, and of a proletarian family dominated by a homophobic father. After a radical break of about thirty years, to such an extent that he did not attend his father's funeral, Eribon came to accept his origins: "It turned out to be much easier for me to write about shame linked to sexuality than about shame linked to class,"[54] he admits with honesty.

Intimate and personal, autobiographical throughout, this essay throws a harsh light on a social world and demonstrates that its author did not need to take off his sociologist's hat to speak about himself. From his experience, Eribon manages to formulate very accurate observations on his own discipline, as, for example, when he returns to the skeptical remarks of Raymond Aron about the elusive character of "class consciousness," a concept he considered to be contestable. What seems incontestable, on the other hand, to the author of *Returning to Reims*, is the bourgeois class consciousness of Aron himself, denied because naturalized: "People in a dominant class position do not notice that they are positioned, situated, within a specific world (just as someone who is white isn't necessarily aware of being so, or someone heterosexual)." Aron's remarks on class consciousness, concludes Eribon, are no more than "the naïve confession offered by a person of privilege who imagines he is writing sociology when all he is doing is describing his own social status." They only met once, but that was enough for him: "[I] immediately felt a strong aversion towards him. The very moment I set eyes on him, I loathed his ingratiating smile, his soothing voice, his way of demonstrating how reasonable and rational he was, everything about him that displayed his bourgeois *ethos* of decorum and propriety, of ideological moderation."[55] An ideological moderation that could also take on inflamed tones when he came to analyzing the class struggle. Eribon's contempt runs deep: "Basically, his pen was for hire: he was a soldier in the service of those in power helping them to maintain their power."[56] The sociologist's autobiographical account thus sets very clear boundaries within his discipline.

About ten years later, another sociologist, Nathalie Heinich, also a former student of Bourdieu who had split from her teacher, published her autobiography, *Une histoire de France* (2018).[57] Richly illustrated, her book is a peaceful text, without anger; it is the story of her family, Jewish on the side of her father, Lionel, from a line of Ukrainian Jews who emigrated to Oran and then settled in Marseille, and Protestant on the side of her mother, Geneviève, from the Alsatian bourgeoisie. This meeting was not straightforward and encountered a lot of resistance from the respective families: the book traces its genealogy in the form of a family album. In her postface, Heinich explains the title: a "history of France," with a small *h*, meaning a "little fragment" rather than a metonymy. Two emblematic stories that intersect with a national history: a history of France among others, "at the level of an individual."[58] Once again, the author claims her ambition to write a family history at the crossroads of sociology and literature. She draws her sources from family archives (administrative documents, photos, testimonies, her own memories), but interprets them with "tools for understanding the world from sociology,"[59] in particular the notions of social mobility, cultural and economic capital, and the dialectic of established/outsider relations borrowed from Norbert Elias.[60] By choosing a mode of intimate expression, she takes the pathway of an "atypical literary genre,"[61] thriving in the company of numerous authors, including W. G. Sebald and Daniel Mendelsohn.

Part-autobiography is taken up in all of Nicole Lapierre's books, at least since *Le silence de la mémoire* (1989), where she set out in the footsteps of the Jews of Płock, the village of Poland where her father was from.[62] Her life, her parents, the past and the present of her family are also at the origin of *Changer de nom* (1995), which explores the onomastic metamorphoses among immigrants, in particular Jews, Armenians, and Arabs, and of *Causes communes* (2011), which rediscovers the history of encounters between Jews and Blacks born out of the struggle against shared oppression.[63] All these works recognize their share of subjectivity but rigorously respect the rules of sociological and anthropological inquiry. *Sauve qui peut la vie* (2015), on the other hand, is an autobiographical narrative in the strict sense of the term.[64] It was born out of a an experience of grief, the suicides of her mother and sister, but it is not an overwhelming story of mourning, suffering, or melancholy regret. It does not seek compassion; quite often, to the contrary, it gives rise to a kind of joyful and invigorating empathy. The cycle has ended; memory is located resolutely on the side of life. It is therefore, as she writes, an "intimate, family story," a register she had "hitherto refused." And if this intimate story is part of a general trend, it is not a conformist text, subject to zeitgeist, written to reinforce an order that would like to draw the moral endorsement of its actions out of memory. After having "crossed the Jewish struggle for memory," in the wake of family history and with the tools of her discipline, she explains why today, in this memory, she no longer "finds herself." Her own memory is not that of lamentation or resentment, but rather that of "a past full of the present that invites the succession of generations."[65] This passage to writing the self, to a fully assumed literary "I," did not happen without going through methodological reflection. In an interview with Jablonka from 2010, she already explained this choice:

to assume the "I" is not, she said, to show "shamelessness or self-absorption, it is to accept the reality of an implication: we are pushed, attracted, by certain subjects of study and research, which are never really chosen by chance." Consequently, writing in the first person seems to her a "rigorous and honest" process, a way "to objectify the part of subjectivity in the research."[66] Coherent with her approach, Nicole Lapierre has made the collection of essays that she edits, "Un ordre d'idées," a place to welcome autobiographies of engaged intellectuals or research interspersed with autobiographical accounts.[67]

Chapter Five

DISCOURSE ON METHOD

IN A methodological essay with an almost programmatic title, *History Is a Contemporary Literature* (2018), Jablonka theorized the new subjectivist genre that interests us here. This plea for a new encounter between history and literature, after the great divorce pronounced in the nineteenth century, is neither the recognition of an alleged superiority of literature over history, according to the postulates of Balzacian realism, nor a challenge to the place of history in the humanities. On the contrary, he instead calls for an *Aufhebung*, a dialectical sublation of this separation, which, in his eyes, is meaningless and harmful. According to Jablonka, the skeptical challenge of postmodernism has damagingly forced history to once again define itself as "science" *against* literature, but, once the wave of the linguistic turn has run its course, he believes the time has come to restore its literary dimension. "History is literature when it is nothing other than itself," he emphasizes. It is not about inserting facts into a narrative or adding "flesh" or ambience to a demonstration, but rather about "the activation of fictions within a line of reasoning that a text materializes and deploys."[1] If the events he studies, the witnesses to whom he listens, the sources he discovers, the documents he examines, the archives he explores fascinate and move him, the historian must be able to transmit his emotions to readers. He does not need to disown himself to give a literary character to his account of the past, as he can very well wed the objective carefulness of the scholar and the creative subjectivity of the writer.

Far from expressing a form of relativism, this recognition of historical subjectivity, affirms Jablonka, "makes knowledge more objective."[2] This is how he annexes Georges Perec to history and makes of him his own model.[3] And this is how he rehabilitates Michelet's "self-history" (*moi-histoire*), of which he accepts the postulate of the "resurrection" of the dead.[4] Reframing an idea of narrative identity developed by Paul Ricœur,[5] he wants to preserve, as we have seen, a substantial distinction between history (a verified account, attested by empirical and factual evidence) and fiction (a plot produced by the imagination of the author), but he emphasizes that the historian as the novelist *writes*, which is to say that they share the same narrative process. Like the novelist, the historian creates a narrative fabric, but he does not invent anything, insofar as his story is not freed from reality. According to Ricœur, narrative identity is both historical and subjective, because it is located at the intersection of distinct but connected temporalities: the phenomenological time of the "cosmos" and the subjective time of human beings, the historical time of a given society and the interior time of the writer. Narrative identity thus overcomes the dichotomy between the objective, factual definition of a being (*sameness*) and its subjective inscription in the world it inhabits (*ipseity*).

In order to translate narrative identity into a new modality of writing history, Jablonka sketches a typology of the multiple forms of "I" that coexist in his work. First, the "I" of position, which situates the author in an observatory, defines his system of references and his point of view. It involves forms of "self-analysis" and self-contextualization that determine an epistemological posture. Then there is the "I" of method: the historian must present his procedure, formulate his hypotheses, select his sources, and explain how he intends to carry out his research. This presentation of historical reasoning—"the question, the investigation, the research, the demonstration"—indicates the "cognitive path" to follow. Finally, there is the "I" of emotion: the historian must give free rein to his feelings and show the existential implication of his investigation. He should not obscure his reactions to the events he describes, but rather inject them into his account as stages that mark the progress of his inquiry.[6] These multiple "I"s are the means of acquiring a greater critical distance from historical actors and events. Jablonka theorizes this method by defining it as a transition from "me" to "I": no longer a hermeneutic of oneself but a research carried out from beginning to end by an "I" transformed into a narrative device.[7]

This method applies to the aforementioned works, but it remains to be proven that this is really a shift from "me" to "I." The success of these books shows that, far from being rattled or disturbed by this narrative style, readers approve of it, even acclaim it. One might argue that, like novelists, other talented historians have painted historical frescoes of a remarkable literary quality without writing in the first person or exhibiting their emotions in a direct form, without mediations (Isaac Deutscher is the first example that comes to mind). But this is not the point, because the methodological innovation of this writing of history is far from being exclusively stylistic or aesthetic. Essentially, what it reveals is an epistemological shift. If historians have always explored and interpreted the past with the more or less sophisticated tools of their discipline, they now do so on the basis of a subjective interrogation. Now their books no longer try only to answer the question what happened, how, and why, but also—or rather—another question of an existential nature: who am I, from where do I come, what familial or generational ties connect me to the past?

Jablonka is right to point out that the claim of "scientist historiography" to produce objective and "axiologically neutral" knowledge is illusory and misleading. This assessment is not new. Methodological subjectivism, however, is not necessarily the best alternative to the abuses and deadlocks of positivism. The permanent ostentation of historical subjectivity in a narrative that mixes present and past, and in which the narrator occupies the same place as the actors of the story he wishes to reconstitute, presents equally vexing drawbacks. In *Laëtitia*, the succession of Jablonka's "I" narratives is dizzying. Omnipresent, he sometimes wears the clothes of the historian, sometimes those of the writer, sometimes he is a simple citizen scandalized by the political instrumentalization of this episode, and sometimes he tells about his friendly relationship with Jessica's lawyer, who plays an intermediary role by providing photos, letters, and access to Laëtitia's Facebook account. He admires the examining magistrate for his impartiality—"her emotions never invaded her professional realm"[8]—with which he feels strong affinities as a historian, but when he puts on his hat as a writer he gives free rein to his own emotions, praising Laëtitia's beauty and saying how moved he is by her texts, to the point of giving a Flaubertian title to a chapter of his book: "Laetitia is me."[9] By thus multiplying the "I" narratives—the objective investigator, the detached analyst, the witness, the friend, the sensitive writer trying to share his emotions with us—the historian becomes exactly what he did not want to be from the start: a "narrator-God."

While the public and critics have acclaimed *Laëtitia*, a work that has won numerous prizes, the reception by scholars has been more mixed. Philippe Artières, historian of autobiographical writing of the outcasts, reproached the author for his "demagogical" posture and his desire to "speak in the place of the actors of history" by returning them once again to their subaltern status and in "infantilizing" them.[10] Léonore Le Caisne, anthropologist who has notably worked on a highly publicized rape story, the "Gouardo affair," accused the author of *Laëtitia* of bending the rules of the investigation to the demands of the narrative in order to make it more fluid and to not "seize" it up.[11] In other words, to make his writing more appealing, she believes that Jablonka gives up the scientific carefulness of the scholar. Sergio Luzzatto's *Primo Levi's Resistance* received similar criticisms: a dubious selection of witnesses, a unilateral investigation, a sovereign indifference to existing studies on justice implemented within the Resistance, and above all an invasive presence of the author, at the risk of becoming "a parody of Indiana Jones who travels between the Aosta Valley and Monferrato." Transforming his research into pure narrative and staging himself as a character in his own history, Luzzatto would thus have ended up favoring fiction "at the expense of the search for historical truth."[12]

In short, in the works of Jablonka and Luzzatto, the narrative prevails over the investigation and directs it by giving rise to "methodical fictions" with purely literary purposes. This annoys some scholars who, faced with the same problems, have bent to the imperatives of inquiry, sometimes by sacrificing the narrative fluidity of the text, sometimes by modestly withdrawing themselves before the voices of witnesses. The problem, of course, is not that these two authors tried to exceed the limits fixed two centuries ago for historical writing, as their intention is not to replace history with literary fiction. The problem is that, in the name of their legitimate literary vocation, historians occupy the stage and overexpose their own "I," the consequences of which are not always fruitful. The problem, in other words, is not the literary ambition of historians—some history books are works of art—but rather the fact that the "literarization" of history authorizes, in a sense, invasion of the account. The past is thus found engulfed under the subjectivity of the one who narrates it. There are two heroes in *Primo Levi's Resistance*, Luzzatto and Primo Levi, as well as in *Laëtitia*, Jablonka and Laëtitia Perrais.

Fifteen years ago, Carlos Forcadell observed a transition in historical studies moving from "class to identity."[13] Today one might make a similar diagnosis speaking about the movement from collective identities to individual identities. Needless to add, such a change redefines the profile of a discipline for which, until recently, adopting the autobiographical form was strictly prohibited. The gap between this new subjectivist approach and previous historiographical currents—think only of the structuralism of Fernand Braudel—is striking. Confronted with the historical temporality of geographical spaces, demography, the economy, and the tectonic movements of human societies, individual temporality evaporates and relegates the "self" to the sphere of the ephemeral or even the anecdotal. As we know, Braudel despised the "event" in which he saw only "surface agitation, the waves which the tides make rise with their powerful movement" and that disappear after reaching the shore.[14] The new subjectivist story, on the other hand, is completely based on an existential temporality. An existential double temporality—that of the actors of the past and that of the historian who brings them back to life—but, all the same, a subjective temporality that takes over and transforms the symphony of great collective dramas into solos. Undoubtedly, histories written from the perspective of the *longue durée* have not disappeared—one need only think of the great nineteenth-century narratives by Christopher Bayly and Jürgen Osterhammel, or those of the twentieth century by Dan Diner, Tony Judt, and Ian Kershaw[15]—but the new subjectivist historical genre is becoming increasingly important. Some historians move easily from one register to another: Mark Mazower, the author of *What You Did Not Tell*, owes his reputation to his works on the history of the twentieth century written in a more conventional style,[16] and Philippe Artières has not had (or has had more moderate) recourse to a homodiegetic style to write on the uses and significance of the banner or on the invention of graphic delinquency.[17]

History is always written in the present, which forges the historians' gaze and constitutes the premise of their "historiographical pact" with the past, namely the recognition of the distance that separates them from their object of study. The subjectivist writing of history is *presentist* because it introduces the "autobiographical pact"—according to the canonical definition of Philippe Lejeune, a writing that assumes "the identity of the author, the narrator, and the protagonist"[18]—in the reconstruction of the past. The two temporalities—that of the author and that of their object—remain distinct, but they always intersect. As a result of these collisions between past and present, authors become hero of the story they are telling, just like those whose journeys they want to retrace. Here too, in Lejeune's words, there is a double "referential pact" because reality and "the verification test" apply to the two intertwined accounts.[19] Strictly speaking, there is no fiction in the author who stages himself or in his account of the past. In family histories (Jablonka, Mazower), the fusion of the two narratives takes on a postmemorial character insofar as it operates a transmission of experiences between generations and reestablishes a connection that has been mangled by the upheavals of history.

Writing history without hiding or sublimating one's "self" also comes with risks. The danger to which this practice most often exposes the historian is, of course, that of sterile narcissism: detractors of the autobiographical genre are sometimes right on target. Articulating historical, sociological, or political analysis and autobiographical narrative is one thing. Replacing the first with the second is another. This slippage is a diffuse temptation to which even the most inspired scholars might yield. In the spring of 2015, just a few months after the terrorist attacks in Paris, Patrick Boucheron penned a short essay with the writer Mathieu Riboulet entitled *Prendre dates*.[20] It is not meaningless that, faced with a traumatic event that has aroused a strong collective reaction on the scale of an entire nation, a historian immediately feels the need to ally with a novelist to write and publish a *journal intime* in which what has just happened is approached only through the prism of emotions. The authors describe the feeling of helplessness that grips them during the days following the attacks and their impression of having fallen into a "dark night" where nothing is any longer intelligible. Their brief essay attempts to express this "numbness of disaster" which affects them and "the escort of stupefaction which suddenly bent their souls."[21] The effect of "shock" by the event is underlined to such an extent over the pages that any effort of rational understanding seems replaced by a sort of ecstasy of dread. As they note a few months later in an interview with *Liberation*, they "experienced the intimate collapse of this barrier between personal mourning and collective emotion," a sensation in which they believed they felt "the breath of history."[22] An essay, in short, to say that they do not understand anything about what happened: "We think everything and its opposite, we listen, we look, we read, we think that everyone is right and the moment after that everyone is wrong."[23] In short, "we remain frozen, dazed" before the images broadcast on the television.[24] The only critical, sincere reflection concerns the causes of such a deep feeling of powerlessness: by selecting their targets, terrorists attack values that, according to Boucheron and Riboulet, "we sincerely believe we want to defend, but that in reality we no longer defend because we do not like them."[25]

If intellectuals once followed Spinoza's motto, "Neither laugh nor cry, but understand," today they seem to want only to cry. This is a rather strange approach: writing about the attacks not to try to interpret them or to analyze the reactions to them—which Emmanuel Todd did in *Who Is Charlie?* (2016)[26]—but solely to express a state of mind. And to register their thoughts in a diary intended not to remain on their desk or in a drawer, but to be published as an "instant book" three months later.

Such an approach runs great risk of substituting emotions for reason and can lead to accepting, if not amplifying, a fear that is easy to instrumentalize. According to Manuel Valls, head of government at the time, "to explain is already wanting to excuse a little." Thus, instead of trying to understand where the horror arose, to question the order that produced it, and to critically analyze the reactions to it, intellectuals take up their pens to say that they feel helpless. Nicolas Vieillescazes bluntly stigmatized this abdication of function: "Thus, the intellectual internalizes his own relegation: integrating the reproach that is often made—of being useless—one makes oneself decorative."[27] The intellectual's voice becomes mere background noise, like music made to create ambience in department stores. The "ambient intellectual" neutralizes critical thinking. What then is left? A diary written as if taking a selfie, a self-portrait for immediate distribution among friends and followers.

It is interesting to compare *Prendre dates* to another hot take, that of Houria Bouteldja, on the massacres perpetrated by Mohamed Merah in Toulouse in March of 2012. Not hiding her emotion or anger, with words that show to what extent this event recalls her past, her own experience, she nevertheless tries to understand: "I cannot deny it. I cannot escape from it. I cannot dig a hole to hide in until it passes. Mohamed Merah is me. The worst thing is that it is true. Like me, he is of Algerian origin, like me, he grew up in a suburb, like me he is a Muslim. . . . Mohamed Merah is me. Mohamed Merah is me, and I am him. We are of the same origin, but above all of the same condition. We are postcolonial subjects." Like her, Merah grew up in suburban neighborhoods turned into social and ethnic ghettos; like her, after September 11, 2001, he felt stigmatized by Islamophobia, by secularism brandished as a weapon against Islam and by racism camouflaged in defense of republican values. Obviously, this neither explained nor justified his crimes, but illuminates the background. "Mohamed Merah, it is me and it is not me," she adds, because by attacking the "French" and the "Jews," essentialized, mythified, and finally transformed into scapegoats, he had "joined the camp of its own enemies."[28] Instead of imprisoning herself in fear and astonishment, Bouteldja tries to understand and wonders about ways to turn rage and resentment into political action, liberating them from nihilistic blindness. Like Boucheron, she writes, in shock, an intimate story addressed to the public. But their reactions are quite different from each other: that of the historian remains locked in the exposure of one's own powerlessness, while that of the young activist tries to turn fear and pain into an attempt to understand and conscious engagement.

Chapter Six

MODELS

HISTORY BETWEEN FILM AND LITERATURE

ANY HISTORICAL narrative with a literary vocation has models. In this regard, a flagship, recognized as a true paradigm by many authors, is the film by Claude Lanzmann, *Shoah* (1985). Its impact has been enormous because, by shaking our representations of the extermination of European Jews, it has modified the relationship between history and memory in the public sphere as well as in the humanities. It has also upset traditional ways of recounting the past, bringing the singularity of the victims into the historian's workshop. In short, a major methodological mutation. It will not be necessary here to present this famous nine-hour film, which gives a voice to the actors of the Holocaust, the great majority victims, but rather to observe the conception of history that irrigates it, giving a new role not only to the subjectivity of those who experienced this trauma but also to the author who interrogates them. The very title—*Shoah* means "catastrophe" in Hebrew, a word unknown at the time outside of Israel—designates a new object, more complex than that of all previous films on Nazi violence.

After Lanzmann's movie, mass extermination ceased to be an abstract and elusive category and became a wound inflicted on real beings in their bodies and spirit. The scholarly concepts usually employed to define this historical experience—fascism, totalitarianism, genocide, barbarism, "self-destruction of reason," dialectic of the Enlightenment, etc.—suddenly seemed hollow in front of these testimonies, this stifling accumulation of suffering. This is the indisputable force of *Shoah*, which has lifted women and men out of anonymity and placed them at the center of a cataclysm that has overturned our perception of history. Far from the linearity of traditional historical reconstructions, this film shows the past as an anthropological laboratory built on a constellation of unique human lives. Certainly, it would not be wrong to consider it as the inaugural moment of a "lachrymal" representation of Jewish history,[1] but this is more due to the reception of the film—and that also applies to certain productions of the new subjectivist history—than to its conception.

Retrospectively, *Shoah* comes as a key moment in the emergence of memory in Western culture (its release roughly coincides with the publication of Yosef Hayim Yerushalmi's *Zakhor*, Pierre Nora's *Realms of Memory*, and Primo Levi's *The Drowned and the Saved*).[2] While Yerushalmi studies the advent of Jewish historiography in the nineteenth century, in the wake of Emancipation, as the end of a transmission of the past entrusted exclusively to collective memory, Lanzmann places memory at the heart of twentieth-century Jewish experience.

While Nora bases his historiographical enterprise on the idea of the end of all transmissible experience—"realms of memory" arise when "milieus of memory" disappear—Lanzmann captures or creates one of these milieus, dispersed and fragmentary, wounded and silent, just before its extinction. And unlike Primo Levi, who weaves a retrospective, reflexive, and critical remembrance, Lanzmann pitches a "literal" recollection to the spectators, that of a past "relived" and, at least in appearance, still intact in the memories of its witnesses.

Shoah greatly contributed to giving the twentieth century the status of an era of violence and genocide. It opened a breach that allowed us to briefly enter into the emotional universe of those who experienced it and to touch a fragment of their shattered lives, but it did not help us to understand or to develop a critical view of the past. In fact, Lanzmann never sought to understand. He claimed an epistemological posture that was summed up by this motto borrowed from an SS guard at Auschwitz, "Here there is no why" (*Hier ist kein warum*),[3] a final sentence reported by Primo Levi in *If This Is a Man* (1947). But unlike Levi, who cited it as emblematic proof of the insanity that reigned in the Nazi camps, Lanzmann appropriated and claimed it as the only valid epistemological principle in the face of National Socialism. After writing that Auschwitz remained a "black hole" for him, Primo Levi nonetheless devoted his life to trying to penetrate and illuminate it. As a man of science and defender of the Enlightenment, he could not give up this effort to understand. Lanzmann, on the contrary, seemed to want only to look at the immeasurable and incomprehensible nature of the Holocaust. From his point of view, trying to understand was "absolute obscenity." "Not to understand," he wrote, "was my ironclad rule during all the years *Shoah* was in the making: I braced myself on this refusal as the only possible attitude, at once ethical and operative. Keeping my guard high up, wearing these blinders, and this blindness itself, were the vital condition of creation."[4] Despite its seriousness and sobriety—bare, unadorned testimonies (though sometimes carefully staged)—*Shoah* inaugurated more than a decade of overflowing rhetoric, quickly fixed in memorial kitsch, around the incomprehensible and unrepresentable character of the Holocaust. Paradoxically, Lanzmann's anthropological approach, based on the collection of testimonies, joins the famous hyperbole of Elie Wiesel who postulates the metaphysical nature—transcending history and therefore unfathomable—of the Nazi genocide.

For Lanzmann, the Holocaust can be neither understood nor interpreted; it can only be narrated by the testimony of the victims. But memory is not an object that can be grasped simply by placing a microphone before the mouths of those who hold it. For Lanzmann, it must be engendered by reviving, in the same place, the trauma suffered. The transmission of this experience transcends all historical account, and the testimony implies a kind of reincarnation. Shoshana Felman, who theorized this conception with the enthusiastic approval of Lanzmann himself, defines *Shoah* as a "unique enactment [in the theatrical sense] by the living witness," which because it takes place on a primal stage (sometimes real, sometimes reconstituted), "is itself *part of a process of realization* of historic truth."[5] As Dominick LaCapra rightly points out, this is what psychoanalysis calls "acting-out," a process that absolutizes and sanctifies the trauma by preventing its working through. In this case, the "reincarnation" does not respond to any "why," but is limited to saying "how" by evacuating all effort at critical understanding.[6]

Shoah is a succession of dialogues between, on the one hand, the actors, witnesses, and victims of the Holocaust and, on the other, Lanzmann—the filmmaker as narrator, interviewer, and investigator, according to the definition proposed by Felman— who therefore becomes a sort of *redeemer*, a central figure in this process of reincarnation of the past. In *History Is a Contemporary Literature*, Jablonka takes up Lanzmann's "blindness," his "refusal to represent" and his "obstinacy in not understanding" to make him a model of his methodological "I."[7] Compared to Jablonka's "I," Lanzmann's is rather ascetic—he never lets go of his coldness and hides his emotions—but in both cases the truth and the deeper meaning of the story are achieved by putting in place a symbiotic relationship between the inquirer (the filmmaker or the historian) and his sources (the witnesses and the archives), even if Lanzmann addresses living beings and Jablonka is in dialogue with the dead.

The equivalent of Lanzmann's narrative model in a graphic novel is Art Spiegelman's *Maus* (1986 and 1991).[8] The animal allegory of the Holocaust in which the Nazis are cats, the Jews are mice, and the Polish are pigs has enjoyed worldwide success. This is not a story of the extermination of the Jews, but rather of the testimony of Vladek, survivor of Auschwitz, father of the narrator, collected during the 1970s at Vladek's house in Queens, and in the Spiegelmans' country house in the Catskills (another ironic allusion to the animal embodied by the Nazis in the story). Autobiography of the author nested in the biography of his father, *Maus* unfolds like the story of a story, because the comic strip shows us their meetings, the recordings, the testimony interrupted at times by fatigue, at times by tasks and the mundane accidents of everyday life.

Spiegelman published his book after his father's death, drawing on his memories, personal archives, and records of their encounters. His book therefore tells both a life and an investigation, and the author reveals himself as much as his father, since he develops his "postmemory" and grief: the mourning of his mother, Anja, who committed suicide in 1968. Both temporalities—that of the author-narrator and that of his father—permanently intersect in the allegorical representation of mice. This mimesis goes beyond transforming Jews into mice, as it also characterizes Art's complex relationship with his father, a simultaneously empathetic and contradictory link, marked by a permanent and insoluble tension between identity and alterity.[9] It is unveiled in the second volume of *Maus* (1991), where the author is seen in the midst of drawing, in profile, with his human features, but wearing a mouse mask. The chapter entitled "Time Flies" brings together the two temporalities of the narrative: "Vladek started working as a tinman in Auschwitz in the spring of 1944. . . . I started working on this page at the very end of February 1987."[10]And further: "In May 1987 Françoise and I are expecting a baby. . . . Between May 16, 1944, and May 24, 1944, over 100,000 Hungarian Jews were gassed in Auschwitz."[11] He thus confesses to Françoise his childhood nightmares, when he imagined the SS coming to round up all the Jewish schoolchildren, and the complete empathy that links him to his father: "I somehow wish I had been in Auschwitz with my parents so I could really know what they lived through."[12] This world-famous graphic novel has certainly contributed, like *Shoah*, to the diffusion of a narrative model based on the autobiographical account of the investigation.

■ ■ ■

Since subjectivist writing of history aims to be literary, it is not surprising to see that it finds many fictional equivalents from which it happens to draw its models. Like Jablonka, Sergio Luzzatto recognizes, in his latest study, that his archetypes are more "ambitiously literary" than "judiciously historiographical," contrary to what the rules of his discipline would like.[13] His last book, *Max Fox*, devoted to the bibliophile forger and book thief Massimo de Caro, strongly recalls Javier Cercas's *Impostor* on the false anarchist fighter and false survivor of Flossenbürg Enric Marco Batlle, but he also cites Emmanuel Carrère, the author of *Limonov*.[14]

The fundamental, almost canonical model for subjectivist writing of history, however, remains W. G. Sebald. His ingredients are known: omnipresence of memory, mourning and melancholy, the direct implication of the author in his stories, the investigation as a narrative device and a recurring use of archival materials, notably photographic, placed in the text not as simple illustrations or embellishments, but rather as crucial pieces that give it a rhythm and create moments of suspension in which the past appears fixed and immobile. In *The Emigrants* (1992), *The Rings of Saturn* (1995), and *Austerlitz* (2001),[15] history, embodied in characters inspired by figures that the author actually encountered, intersects with the memory of the narrator, who sometimes goes into long digressions in his own memories. The pathways of exile mingle with the itinerary of a German who emigrates to England to flee the hypocrisy and weight of postwar forgetful Germany. Sebald's writing advances balanced on the ridgeline between exploration of the past and an erratic, contemplative identity quest. The heroes of *The Emigrants* are all outsiders, exiles, and melancholic. Two of them are Jews the author met in Manchester, Dr. Henry Selwyn and Max Ferber; the third, Paul Breyter, who had to flee Germany in the 1930s due to the anti-Semitic laws of the Third Reich, was his teacher; and the fourth, Ambros Adelwarth, was his uncle, who emigrated to the United States where he died in Ithaca, in the state of New York. Some characters are fictional or do not appear under their real names.

Sebald called his texts "fictions in prose." On the one hand, in an interview, he affirmed that 90 percent of the photos included in his book were authentic.[16] On the other hand, the portraits of emigrants are also self-portraits, as their stories unfold in the narrative of encounters that are as much opportunities for the narrator to speak about himself and to deliver to the reader his own reflections on his life and story. *Austerlitz*, the most ambitious of his novels, is another portrait of exile, that of Jacques Austerlitz, an accomplished architectural historian, botanist, and photographer, whom the narrator met in the Antwerp train station. Austerlitz grew up in a Puritan family, which provided him with a rigorous education, in England where he arrived in 1939 with the last train of Jewish children who had been able to leave Czechoslovakia at the time of the German invasion. Like *The Emigrants*, *Austerlitz* is a narrative where the life that the narrator wants to elucidate blends with the story of his own life in a permanent entanglement between reality and fiction, past and present.

As Mark Anderson so aptly notes, there is an astonishing parallel between Sebald and Lanzmann, because both, despite their opposing styles, make their interlocutors speak: Lanzmann with his ostentatious, commanding, and invasive presence; Sebald as a discreet investigator and reserved listener.[17] This modesty is probably due to the fact that Sebald was born in Germany in 1944. His Germanness is the source of a "guilt" that prompted him to emigrate; he feels it as a poison that eats away at him from within, but it is also the underground motor of his books (with some exceptions, such as the story of "homecoming" in *Vertigo*, it is only rarely verbalized).[18] Modesty creates a strange symbiotic relationship between the author and his characters. In *The Emigrants*, Ferber describes Germany with striking words that echo those of the narrator, as the two men have fled their native country and feel a sort of enigmatic and inexplicable dread toward it that time has not attenuated:

> There is neither a past nor a future. At least, not for me. The fragmentary scenes that haunt my memories are obsessive in character. When I think of Germany, it feels as if there were some kind of insanity lodged in my head. Probably the reason why I have never been to Germany again is that I am

afraid to find that this insanity really exists. To me, you see, Germany is a country frozen in the past, destroyed, a curiously extraterritorial place, inhabited by people whose faces are both lovely and dreadful.[19]

Ferber's long monologue turns into a reflection by Sebald on the unsettling connection that links him to his own country. The borders between character and author blur. In recounting the life of the first—or rather by making him recount his life— the second speaks to us about himself. At the turn of the twenty-first century, Sebald transforms the relationship between history and literature by inventing a new form of subjective writing that intersects past and present. And this foundational caesura paves the way for other narrators.

Besides Sebald, we must mention two other writers who give literary form to their inquiries into the past: Patrick Modiano and Daniel Mendelsohn. There is no romantic fiction in *Dora Bruder* (1997), a "novel" that tells about Modiano's investigation of a Jewish youth who really existed and whose traces he discovered in an old newspaper.[20] This book reconstructs a unique, unknown, and forgotten life and inscribes it in the memory of its author. An announcement of a few lines, published in *Paris-Soir* on December 31, 1941, by the parents of Dora, who had just run away, incites the narrator to retrace, fifty years later, the ephemeral pathway of a life that coincides with a historical tragedy: the runaway was deported and killed in Auschwitz like her parents. This shattered existence takes shape in the author's remembrance and resurges in an urban landscape made up of real places: streets, boulevards, and buildings, the neighborhood of Modiano's youth.[21] The author first follows his investigation to the civil registrar of the 12th arrondissement of Paris, then to the courts, and finally to the archives of the Saint-Coeur-de-Marie boarding school, where Dora was placed after her first flight, as well as those of the boarding school of Tourelles, which was her last known residence. The author also consulted Dora's school registers, and he even managed to find her in the archives of the General Union of French Jews (UGIF), the Jewish institution created by the Vichy authorities under the Occupation, preserved at the Yivo Institute in New York.

For Modiano, Dora Bruder is a bit like the older sister he never had, as he was, like her, a runaway youth. The adolescent adventures remind him of his own and spark spontaneous, immediate empathy:

I remember the intensity of my feelings while I was on the run in January 1960—an intensity such as I have seldom known. It was the intoxication of cutting all ties at a stroke: the clean break, deliberately made, from enforced rules, boarding school, teachers, classmates; you have nothing to do with these people from now on; the break from your parents, who have never understood you, and from whom, you tell yourself, it's useless to expect any help; feelings of rebellion and solitude carried to flash point, taking your breath away and leaving you in a state of weightlessness. . . . I think of Dora Bruder. I remind myself that, for her, running away was not as easy as it was for me, twenty years later, in a world that had once more been made safe. To her, everything in that city of December 1941, its curfews, its soldiers, its police, was hostile, intent on her destruction. At sixteen years old, without knowing why, she had the entire world against her.[22]

Beyond the memories triggered by the adventures of this adolescent, Modiano is also moved by a desire for knowledge; he wants to paint the portrait of Dora Bruder, extract her from oblivion, capture a few moments of her ephemeral existence, bring her traces to light. It is in this sense that Susan R. Suleiman sees in this story a good example of "empathic identification": not an appropriation, but an affinity that engenders a true work of knowledge of the other.[23] The fate of Dora Bruder haunted Modiano for a number of years, as the announcement published in *Paris-Soir* had already inspired him in an earlier novel, *Honeymoon* (1990), where, however, the name of the young girl was changed to be integrated into a purely fictional story.[24] *Dora Bruder*, on the contrary, does not want to stray from the factual base that is its source. The result is a vision of history that, despite its anchoring and its fidelity to reality, is born from the desire to save what has disappeared. Instead of revealing the past, the sources—documents, archives, "evidences," one would say in the legal lexicon—allow access to it; they are remainders, remnants, fragments of what has happened that we can use to recompose a landscape, to give form to a substance that is no more. The place of investigation in this novel and the author's empathy for his character also announce and prepare for the subjectivist turn in history that is the question of these pages.

Daniel Mendelsohn's *The Lost* (2006) is not a novel either, in
the strict sense of the word. It is a family saga and an investigation into the life of Shmiel Jäger, the author's grandfather's
brother.[25] A butcher by profession, the great-uncle was born in
Bolechow, a small town in the Habsburg Empire (now in
Ukraine), and lived there with his wife and their four daughters, whose beauty aroused the admiration of all. Intrigued by
the air of resemblance to his great-uncle attributed to him while
at family gatherings in New York, Mendelsohn searched the
archives and met several Jews from Bolechow who had survived
the Holocaust, in Australia, Denmark, Sweden, and Israel, to
reconstruct the past of his family. He eventually went to
Bolechow itself, where he found the house in which his great-
uncle lived, the site where he was captured before being killed
by the Einsatzgruppen in October of 1941. Like Jablonka's
books, *The Lost* is punctuated with images and, after having
described his investigation, Mendelsohn shares with the reader
the series of questions that accompanied him during the writing of his book: how to reconstruct the history of a family, but,
above all, how to recount it? "How to be a narrator?": this, for
Mendelsohn, is the real problem facing his generation.[26] It is
therefore a question of transmission of the postmemory of those
who were born after the war; in order to attempt to answer it,
the author had to confront another: how to tell history? This is
the question of the relationship between history and literature.
In the note that closes *The Lost*, Mendelsohn makes this clari-
fication: "The events recorded in this book are true. All formal
interviews were recorded on videotape, and nearly all other
conversations, including telephone conversations, were either

recorded by the author or reconstructed on the basis of notes taken by the author during these conversations."[27] Such concern for veracity generally characterizes the work of the investigator or historian, not that of the novelist. But now they all seem to follow similar processes.

Chapter Seven

HISTORY AND FICTION

THE HISTORICAL novel experienced a new golden age a few years after Sebald's sudden death in 2001, but a literary creation like *The Name of the Rose* (1980) by Umberto Eco had already brought together the essential ingredients of this new wave: a plot based on a vast documentation and sequence of events in the form of an investigation or a police procedural.[1] Nourished by staggering erudition on monastic life and the culture of the Middle Ages, from theological quarrels to herbalist treatises, the logical deductions of Guillaume de Baskerville, a veritable Sherlock Holmes of the fourteenth century investigating in a Benedictine monastery in Piedmont, assisted by the narrator, the novice Adso de Melk, are filled with references both literary (notably "The Library of Babel" by Jorge Luis Borges) and political, going back to Italy in the 1970s (with the supporters of communist orthodoxy embodied by the bishops of the Inquisition and the revolutionaries of the extraparliamentary left painted as Dolcinean heretics). However, it was in the 2000s that the literary phenomenon prefigured by Eco gained momentum.

At the origin of this revival of the historical novel, there is undoubtedly a change in the period that shifted the twentieth century from the present to the past—a closed past, henceforth susceptible to being historicized—and gave an unprecedented depth to individual and collective memory. But there is also a dissatisfaction with the historiographical discourse that was dominant at the time. The century that had just passed was too charged with passions, emotions, and sufferings to be entrusted to the "anesthetizing" work of historians. It also demanded other approaches, including that of literature. Undoubtedly favored by the exhaustion of a long cycle dominated by the nouveau roman, which posited the capacity of literature to draw its sources and materials from language itself, writers' return to the real found in France a privileged space where the latter sometimes reinvented the historical novel and sometimes sought new hybrid forms by mixing history and literature. However, the phenomenon concerns all languages and epochs.

Many works of this resurgence of the historical novel, including international best sellers, deal with National Socialism, World War II, and the Holocaust. They merit special attention, in the context of this study, because of their contiguity with the new subjectivist writings of history. The most famous of these novels is undoubtedly *The Kindly Ones* (2006) by Jonathan Littell.[2] Constructed as the memoirs of a former SS officer, Maximilien Aue, involved in the Nazi crimes on the Eastern Front, this novel features, in more than eight hundred pages, almost all crucial moments of the war and the Holocaust, from Babi

Yar to Stalingrad, from Majdanek to Sobibor, scrolling through
an incredible gallery of Nazi hierarchs, officers, doctors, law-
yers, and camp leaders of the Third Reich. Three years after *The
Kindly Ones*, Yannick Haenel published *The Messenger*, portrait
of the courier of the Polish government in exile who, during the
war, visited the Warsaw Ghetto and then informed the Allies,
during a meeting with Roosevelt in 1943, of the extermination
of the Jews.[3] For twenty years, a literary wave has been unfolding in Spain, centered on the Civil War and its aftermath. Its
main representative is Javier Cercas, who dissected the dilemmas and passions, commitment and remorse, repressions and
memory linked to the history of Francoism. Rejecting the char-
acterization as historical novelist, Cercas presents himself
rather as a writer interested in studying the presence of the past
in the memory of his contemporaries.[4] In Germany, the famous
critic and essayist Hans Magnus Enzensberger devoted an
unclassifiable work to Kurt von Hammerstein, the Reichswehr
general who decided to resign in 1934 to assert his opposition
to Hitler. *The Silences of Hammerstein* is neither a novel—the
author did not want to publish it under this label—nor, strictly
speaking, a biography, because his narration of Hammerstein's
life is enriched by "posthumous conversations" with the actors
of his time as well as "glosses" that deepen and interpret the different dimensions of his historical tableau: the Prussian aristocracy, the Weimar crisis, and the advent of National Socialism. Hence the subtitle of his book: "A German Story."[5] More
recently, the historical novel made its return to Italy, where it
reached its climax with a fictional biography of Mussolini, *M.
Il figlio del secolo* (2018), by Antonio Scurati. The first of three

planned volumes, crowned with the most prestigious literary prize on the peninsula, this novel tells the story of the Duce's life between 1919, the year in which his movement was founded, and 1925, that of the transformation of fascism into a political regime.[6]

All these works scrupulously respect the historicity of the events they relate and often of their characters, whom they describe by constructing plausible portraits. They are based on solid historical knowledge and sometimes even on the use of primary sources or archives. Scurati is keen to make this clear at the start of his novel: "The facts and characters in this documentary novel do not surface from the author's imagination. On the contrary, each event, character, dialogue or speech related here is historically documented and/or validly attested by more than one source. That said, the fact remains that history is an invention to which reality contributes its own materials. An invention, however, not arbitrary."[7] Littell displays his knowledge of the history of National Socialism throughout the nine hundred pages of his novel. That begins from the start of the book, where he launches into calculations to determine the number of German, Jewish, and Soviet deaths per hour, per minute, and per second between June 22, 1941, and May 8, 1945, based on the most reliable estimates established by historical research.[8] When he lingers over Heinrich Himmler's famous speech in Poznan in October 1943, in which the leader of the SS presented the extermination of the Jews as proof of the moral superiority of National Socialism, he even authorizes himself, through the lips of the narrator, to clarify details from the archives with obsessional precision: "The October 4 speech was entered as evidence in the Nuremberg trials, under document number 1919-PS . . .; moreover, it was recorded, either on a wax disk or on a red oxide magnetic tape—the historians aren't in agreement, and on this point I cannot enlighten them."[9] The hero of *The Kindly Ones*, Maximilien Aue, whose adventures are a complete repertoire of Nazi atrocities, has a purely fictional existence, as with numerous situations in which Yannick Haenel, Leonardo Padura, or Antonio Scurati place their characters: President Roosevelt eyeing the legs of his secretary, Ramón Mercader subjected to the moral and political influence of his mother, or the erotically charged atmosphere of a hotel room in Milan where Mussolini sleeps with his mistress and adviser Margherita Sarfatti.[10]

It is precisely this genre of narrative digression that historian Jablonka says he does not allow himself in his works. Relating the arrest of his grandparents at 17 Passage d'Eupatoria, in Paris, on the morning of February 25, 1943, he holds himself to a strict record of the facts. "I could conjure up the sound of footsteps on the stairs, the loud knock at the door, the rude awakening," he writes, but he wants his narrative "to be incontrovertible, based on evidence or, at least, on hypotheses and deductions." He calls this the "moral contract" of the historian who, therefore, must "embrace these uncertainties as full partners in the complete narrative, while at the same time resisting the lure of pure imagination, however conveniently it serves to fill in the blanks."[11] Further on, nonetheless, when he evokes the end of his grandparents, Jablonka allows himself the fiction that he had previously forbidden: "Matès must be seeing in his mind's eye his mother baking bread, his father reciting the

Canticle of Canticles on the eve of the Sabbath, majestic and luminous in his satin caftan. . . . Matès is watching the opalescent moon: it is hideously beautiful, russet, indifferent to these restless insects doomed to disappear. Matès feels his mind is coming apart, cracked with visions. There are no more free men on this earth."[12] The demand of the literary narrative finally takes the upper hand over the "moral contract" to which the historian is held, who, insofar as wanting to "fictionalize" history, he explains, must not escape reality.

In counterpoint, Laurent Binet reflects on the same questions from the perspective of the writer. Author of a novel on the Czech Resistance attack on Reinhard Heydrich, he notes that, even if they are respectful of the facts, historical novels always leave him unsatisfied because, "in every case, fiction wins out over history."[13] He wanted to write something else that would be both a historical narrative and "a personal affair" in which he narrates the self. The result is what he calls "an *infranovel*,"[14] where the adverb *infra* indicates the relationship between the attack on Heydrich, which he contextualizes and admirably places in the plot, and the narrator—himself—who not only recounts his investigation but delivers his reflections on history and literature, as well as his approach to the past. When Natacha, his partner, reproaches him for inventing his story, he gets annoyed, because he has always denounced "the puerile, ridiculous nature of novelistic invention," but ultimately he does not change his wording: when Himmler learns of Heydrich's death following the attack, "the blood rises to his cheeks and he feels his brain swell inside his skull."[15] His novel, for it is one, is titled *HHhH* (*Himmlers Hirn heißt Heydrich*, meaning "Himmler's brain is called Heydrich"). Further on, Binet is forced to recognize that history and literature cannot dissolve into each other. Here is his observation:

> I'm fighting a losing battle. I can't tell this story the way it should be told. This whole hotchpotch of characters, events, dates, and the infinite branching of cause and effect—and these people, these real people who actually existed. I'm barely able to mention a tiny fragment of their lives, their actions, their thoughts. I keep banging my head against the wall of history. And I look up and see, growing all over it— ever higher and denser, like a creeping ivy—the unmappable pattern of causality.[16]

Therefore, *HHhH* is a novel. Christine Berberich even defines it as "a clever example of postmodern historiographical metafiction."[17] If *A History of the Grandparents I Never Had,* which its publisher presents on the cover as "an investigation," is rich in details, images, evocative situations and emotions, exactly the opposite of a dry and detached story, that does not come about without mediations from the raw material on which the work is based; it is due to the narrator, to his ability to mold the dough of the story without sugarcoating or contaminating it, while nevertheless going beyond the objective and detached narrative of the historian.

The familial and postmemorial quest of two authors like Jablonka and Mendelsohn presents a striking parallel with *Lord of All the Dead* (2017) by Javier Cercas, a new piece of his rereading of the Spanish Civil War. Unlike *Soldiers of Salamis,* the novel that, some fifteen years ago, established his reputation in European letters, this new story is a novel that does not recognize itself as such: it is the reconstruction of the short life of his uncle, Manuel Mena, who was born, like Cercas, in Ibahernando, a small town in Extremadura, enlisted in Franco's army in 1936 at the age of seventeen, and died two years later in the Battle of the Ebro. A portrait of Manuel Mena occupied a place of honor in the living room of the Cercas family home, and the writer decided to "redeem" his uncle, to remove him from the anonymous coldness of this portrait and to restore his life to him, retracing his journey in the most rigorous and factual way possible. So, he immersed himself in the family archives, then in those of the city and the army, and met the last survivors who knew Manuel Mena. To conduct his investigation, Cercas was forced to take off the novelist's hat and put on that of the historian. His book is written in both first and third person, depending on the different levels of storytelling. A story in the first person, when he recounts his investigation and his family relationships, and a presentation in the third person, when, as a narrator, he reconstructs the life and times of his uncle, but also when he speaks of himself as a part of this family picture. Like Mendelsohn and Jablonka, Cercas explains his method:

> I thought that to tell Manuel Mena's story I should tell my own story; or, to put it another way, I thought that in order to write a book about Manuel Mena I should split myself in two: I should tell one story on one side, the story of Manuel Mena, and tell it exactly as a historian would tell it, with a historian's coolness and distance and scrupulous veracity,

confining myself strictly to the facts and disdaining legend and fantasy and the writer's freedom, as if I were not who I am but another person; and, on the other side, I should write not a story but the story of a story—that is, the story of how and why I came to tell the story of Manuel Mena.[18]

Cercas thus follows in the footsteps of his unknown uncle, the uncle he "never had," exactly like Mendelsohn and Jablonka, who battle with the ghosts of ancestors they never knew. His work is a good illustration of what Jablonka calls the "investigative I"—he tells "the story of a story"—and Ginzburg, the "evidential paradigm," since he at times compares himself to "a detective going over a crime scene."[19] As for Matès and Idesa Jablonka, Shmiel Jäger, or even Max and Frouma Mazower, Cercas's book is a sort of redemption of Manuel Mena. At the end of the book, the young officer photographed in a splendid white uniform has again become a human being of flesh and blood, along with his ideals, aspirations, illusions, and disappointments as well. In short, he becomes a person again with his singular life, no longer "a hazy, distant figure for me, as rigid, cold, and abstract as a statue, a mournful family legend reduced to a portrait confined to the dusty silence of a dusty loft of the deserted family home."[20] He ceased to be both the hero and the shame of the family—the hero of his mother and the shame of a family with a Francoist past—to take on more concrete features, those of a "simple self-respecting *muchacho* disillusioned of his ideals and a soldier lost in someone else's war, who didn't know why he was fighting anymore." It is at this point that Cercas's account becomes loaded with pathos: "And then I saw him."[21] The image of Manuel Mena, one might say in quoting a famous essay by Siegfried Kracauer on photography, had ceased to be an "*unredeemed*, ghost-like reality."[22]

Even if the work of Cercas does not present itself as a rehabilitation of Francoism, it is at least a rehabilitation of Manuel Mena, a young fascist. With strong lyricism, Cercas compares his young uncle, a member of the Spanish Falange, to Achilles, thus conferring upon him the status of a mythic hero. His conclusion is interesting because, among other things, it reveals the ambiguities of the "methodological I," which experiences an empathic identification no longer with the victims but rather with the persecutors, with someone who has chosen the wrong camp. The political ambiguity of the *Lord of All the Dead* is therefore deeply linked to the emotional "I" of the author. The transference implemented by Jablonka and Cercas points to different subjects, but their conclusions are quite close: history is a human tragedy in which the actors are irreducibly singular subjects. In two works, which do not hide their simultaneous historical and literary ambitions, they humanize their heroes by removing them from anonymity, but while Jablonka restores a face and a voice to forgotten victims, Cercas transforms a Falangist into a victim, into a human being who, at heart, was neither better nor worse than his enemies. A civil war is a fratricidal conflict, tragic, and in that which bloodied Spain between 1936 and 1939 Republicans and Francoists were essentially interchangeable: this is the wisdom that Cercas had already shown in *Soldiers of Salamis*, his first success. In it he establishes a striking equivalence between the death of Republican poet Antonio Machado in Collioure, on the French-Spanish border, at the end of the civil war, and the failed execution, at the same time, of Rafael Sánchez Mazas, poet and nationalist ideologist, one of the founders of the Falange. There is, however, a difference between the two books that goes beyond simple nuance: in *Soldiers of Salamis* humanity is embodied by Miralles, the young Republican fighter who, in the restless hours of retreat, spares the life of Sánchez Mazas because he feels pity for him, without even knowing his true identity, while in *Lord of All the Dead* this shifts to Manuel Mena, that is to say, to the Falangist himself.

While Jablonka writes to his grandparents, calling them "my beloved gods," Cercas imagines a dialogue with his dying uncle in which he promises to preserve his honor and memory, attempting to convince him that his death has not been useless, that it was worthy and heroic. His cause was bad, but his commitment was nonetheless justified: as in Greek mythology, his death was "a *kalos thanatos* . . . a perfect death that crowned a perfect life."[23]

As many critics have pointed out, Cercas is the emblematic representative of a generation of writers who, by dint of questioning the so-called lapses of memory of the democratic transition after Franco's death, ended up adopting a sort of "equidistance" between the Republic and Francoism, between fascism and antifascism. However, far from being a "neutral" methodological posture, empathy implies a political choice.[24] Describing the Nazi massacres through a narrative in the first person, Littell adopts an ambiguous posture that troubles the reader—according to Dominick LaCapra, he tends to "amalgamate or reverse perpetrator and victim"[25]—but Max Aue's adventures

during the war do not breathe any complacency, while the rehabilitation of Manuel Mena by Cercas is the result of an identification that turns into a historical and political gaze, in this case
an apologetic gaze.

In an interview with Spanish historian Justo Serna, Cercas
admits that his investigation was not, as he claims in his book,
as objective as that of a historian. A tiny dose of invention, he
explains, is enough to build a novel; it can change everything,
"like a drop of poison in a glass of water."[26] He adds, in Littell's
wake, that there is a "literary truth" distinct yet complemen-
tary to "historical truth," a literary truth that he assimilates, in
citing Aristotle, with the moral truth of history.[27] He does not
write historical novels; he writes "novels on the present" in
which he wants to show to what extent the present remains
haunted by the past.[28] All is said. Subjectivist writing of the
past, whether historical or literary, or both at the same time,
does not free itself from the political choices of its author, which
orient and irrigate it. But it does not always assume them; sometimes it serves to mask them. The vision of history that inspires
Lord of All the Dead is the same that, for years, led the political
authorities to organize, on October 12, during Spanish National
Day, parades in which a former Republican appeared, arm in
arm, with a former soldier of the División Azul that Franco sent
to fight on the Eastern Front alongside the German army.

Now let's leave the novel to return to history. Reading Cercas's book, I remembered another autobiographical text that
made a lot of noise in Italy about twenty years ago. In 2000,
Roberto Vivarelli, respected historian of the Normal School of
Pisa, one of the oldest Italian universities, published *La fine di*

una stagione: Memoria 1943–1945, a book in which he revealed
and claimed his past as a young militiaman under the fascist
Republic of Salò. These memoirs had considerable impact and
raised violent controversies. Vivarelli did not defend the fascist
regime—at least that is what he said—but he stubbornly refused
to admit his faults: "I do not regret what I did, and I would be
ready to do it again."[29] He was proud of his youthful political
commitment, and his reasons, he said, were not ideological, but
existential, connected to the history of his family.

His own fascism, he wrote, stemmed from his "desire to
remain faithful to the memory of [his] father" and also from the
fact that, for him, "fascism and homeland were the same thing."
He was aware that the cause of fascism had been "morally and
historically unjust," but he still felt pride in having fought for
his convictions.[30]

Once again, subjectivity advanced rights stronger than any
historical reason. Civil wars are tragedies on both sides of the
barricade. The question is to know whether their interpretation
can stop at this observation. For Vivarelli, that was enough to
take a complacent look at his life and choices. He had chosen
the wrong side, but his commitment had been pure and noble,
like that of Manuel Mena. If history is basically an affair of family *pietas*, it is fidelity that counts, the fate of ancestors and
their actions no longer matter. Whether this piety is directed
at the Jews deported to Auschwitz or the Falangists is only secondary, if not anecdotal. They all become Homeric heroes, and
their descendants, historians or novelists, emulators of Aeneas
carrying his father on his shoulders, according to the image suggested by Jablonka.

This observation does not call into question the legitimacy of the affection one might have for loved ones, whoever they are, nor does it deny the interest of exploring the subjectivity of those who have found themselves on the bad side or made blameworthy choices. The study of the contexts and psychological mechanisms that govern the creation of executioners has allowed real progress in our knowledge of the past and has inspired poignant literary accounts,[31] the interest of which nevertheless lies in their ability to integrate the subjectivity of the actors into a broader and more complex view of the past. However, Cercas and Vivarelli tell us that deep historical meaning lies in this subjectivity, in the fact that the militia members of Salò and the Spanish Falangists were not only human beings just like their enemies, but that they could even express what is most noble in humankind. Once erected as a key to interpreting the past, this approach risks producing other Andreas Hillgruber, the German historian previously mentioned and for whom the soldiers of the Wehrmacht, who defended the borders of the Reich by protecting their families from the "vengeful orgies" of the Red Army, were Homeric heroes of World War II.

Cercas is certainly not nostalgic for Francoism; he is perfectly right to underscore that to understand does not mean to justify and that the mission of literature consists in "exploring the infinite possibilities of the human being," but he still claims his ambition to give a "new and singular vision" of the Spanish Civil War and, when questioned about his "revisionism," his answer hardly differs from that given in the past by Ernst Nolte and Renzo De Felice: any advance in historical knowledge implies calling into question previous conceptions.[32] He thus avoids the fact that what is reproached with "revisionists" is not to have proposed new interpretations of the past or to have rectified erroneous readings, but to have overturned the pillars of a shared historical consciousness, which saw culprits among the fascists, Nazis, and Francoists, and in antifascism one of the premises of postwar democracy. Cercas claims to tackle certain commonplaces of the present—for example, those that allowed Enric Marco to lie for years because he was telling people what they wanted to hear—but Justo Serna is right to note that the success of a novel like *Soldiers of Salamis* can be substantially explained by its adherence to the "moral predispositions of our time," that is to say, the idea that "there is not a camp of partisans of good, above all suspicion, facing evil located in the opposite camp."[33]

In terms of public use of the past, Cercas's literary nonfictions, or "real stories," fuel the cause of historians who, by emphasizing the clairvoyance of an "amnesiac" transition, establish an equivalence between the Popular Front of 1936 and Francoism, thus postulating the benefits of an anti-anti-Francoist liberal democracy.[34] Vivarelli's autobiography, for its part, belonged to the anti-antifascist campaign that was in full swing during the 1990s and led Luciano Violante, member of the Democratic Party and president of the Chamber of Deputies, to laud, in a sensational speech, the "guys from Salò" (*i ragazzi di Salò*), those who in 1943 and 1944 had not chosen the Resistance, but the fascist militia allied with the German occupation forces, whose memory was henceforth carried with pride by the Italian Republic.[35] Such are the avatars of subjectivist writings of the past—as much historian as novelist—that, by flouting the public use of history, believe themselves to grasp its deep meaning by focusing on the lived experience and subjectivity of its actors.

Jablonka, Mendelsohn, and Cercas proceed in an analogous manner, even if their goals and conclusions diverge. They participate in the formulation of a discourse on the past that fits into the present and involves literature as well as history. The resulting hybridization inevitably raises the question again of the boundaries between the two, boundaries being, by definition, meeting places as well as dividing lines. In the introduction to *The Anatomy of a Moment* (2010), his work devoted to the failed coup attempt of February 23, 1981, during the democratic transition of post-Franco Spain, Javier Cercas suggests two levels of reading. He first wanted to write a novel, he explains, but then he realized that fiction would not equal the richness and complexity of reality, and so he decided to tell the latter, abandoning novelistic fiction. The book he wrote is a hybrid: "Although it's not a history book . . . it will not entirely renounce being read as a history book; nor will it renounce answering to itself as well as answering to reality, and from there, although it's not a novel, it won't entirely renounce being read as a novel."[36] Justo Serna claims that by presenting it as a novel his publisher could expect more significant sales figures, but Cercas is right to point out that his work belongs to history as well as to literature, for he remains a novelist even when he writes essays.

About ten or so years ago, the debate centered on *The Messenger*, the aforementioned novel by Yannick Haenel centered on a Polish officer who alerted the Allies to the Holocaust.

Haenel organizes his novel into three clearly separated parts. In the first two, he summarizes Jan Karski's interview with Lanzmann in *Shoah* and the report that he wrote in English in 1944 on his mission in occupied Poland, *Story of a Secret State*,[37] while in the third he transforms the officer into a literary character and makes him describe his meeting with the American president Roosevelt and express, at the end of his life, bitter accounts about his own existence. In an introductory note, Haenel specifies that this third chapter "is a fiction" in which "the phrases and thoughts that he attributes to Jan Karski are invented." This literary mode allows him to denounce the culpable inaction of the Allies in the face of the extermination of the Jews ("Still today, I can hear him stifling a yawn as I spoke about the fate of those Jews who were resisting the Nazis, and the fate of the Jews who were being deported to the death camps to be exterminated"),[38] and to deploy a vision of history in which all is ultimately equivalent ("I had confronted Nazi violence, I had suffered from Soviet violence, and now, completely unexpectedly, I was being introduced to the insidious violence of the Americans.")[39]

He would like to show us the real Karski, beyond the one we know: "At the time when the book was published, in 1944, it was impossible for me to tell the truth. . . . We were counting on the Allies, and so it was necessary not to annoy the Americans, who in turn did not want to fall out with the Soviets, and so I said nothing in my book against either of them."[40] In other words, the real Karski would not be the one in his texts but the one that came from Haenel's pen. Nevertheless, fiction is not above ethics and should not ignore the rights of the dead.[41]

In the violent controversy aroused by his book, Haenel claimed his right, as a writer, to invent dialogues and sketch the profile of his characters, recalling, through a quote from Kafka's *Diaries*, that the vocation of literature is precisely "the assault on borders."[42] He thus replied to Lanzmann who accused him of having falsified historical truth by thinking that "literature and truth have nothing in common and [that] the first does not have to worry about the second."[43] This is a pertinent observation. Considering the omissions by Lanzmann in *Shoah* and in the film he subsequently made on Karski, however, a similar grievance could be addressed to Lanzmann himself.[44]

Both Haenel in his fiction and Lanzmann in editing his film *interpret* Karski. Both, one might say, using Annette Wieviorka's words about the first, "show no respect for the witness whose testimony they hijack."[45] Yet, if we cannot contest the right of a writer to invent characters, we may have reservations about his ability to recreate or to represent the past. This also applies to Haenel, because his fiction is not that of George Steiner, who imagines Hitler in the Amazon jungle thirty years after the Second World War,[46] and even less that of Roberto Benigni, who, in *Life Is Beautiful*, frees the Auschwitz camp with American soldiers, or of Quentin Tarantino, who, in *Inglourious Basterds*, kills Hitler in a Parisian cinema stormed by the Resistance, thus transforming this burlesque finale into an allegory of the primacy of the cinematographic imagination over historical reality. Haenel is not joking, as he seeks to capture the deep meaning of history through fiction.

In this controversy, which already aroused anger over *The Kindly Ones*, and which has punctually resurfaced with Éric

Vuillard's *The Order of the Day* and Scurati's book on Mussolini, historians and novelists seem to be entrenched in two irrec-
oncilable camps. The proponents of historiographical positivism reaffirm their claim to a monopoly of the past by stigmatizing
Haenel's transgression, the "untrue" character of Maximilien
Aue, and the dating errors that punctuate Mussolini's portrait,
as if *The Messenger*, *The Kindly Ones*, and *M* were not novels but
doctoral dissertations.[47] Jean Solchany is right to point out the
limits of historical expertise. Scholars certainly have the right
to express their well-informed opinion on the subject of literary works dealing with their field, but they must do so with pru-
dence, as "the freedom of the novelist and the specificity of his
work are not to be taken carelessly."[48]

With an equally haughty reaction, the writers displayed their
sovereign contempt for criticism concerning the historical "cred-
ibility" of their characters. Thus they claimed their right to
assert a "literary truth" not precisely defined but opposed to
"historical truth." As we have just seen, this is notably the
response of Littell and Cercas to their critics.[49] However,
whereas Littell did not want, in painting the portrait of Max
Aue, to present an archetype of a Nazi officer, but rather to create a fictional character planted in a setting of war, genocide,
and National Socialism, Haenel's fiction features such historical figures as Karski and Roosevelt, which makes his deviations
from known historical facts more troublesome and his portraits
less credible. Scurati, on the other hand, does not contrast any
"literary truth" with historical truth. After admitting the factual errors that mar his novel—a few minor details including
dating errors—he pleaded for "a new alliance between historians

and novelists." He recognizes that without the achievements of historical research his novel could not have been written and adds that, "while being loosely created on a documentary basis, his book is a novel, not a historical essay."[50] Its results may be approved or criticized, but it should not be judged with the criteria that govern a critique of historiographical work. This distinction is obvious, and to not admit it is either to deny the autonomy of history and literature or to infantilize readers who would not be able to see the difference between analysis and fiction.

Sometimes the distinction between the two is made in order to fix hierarchies, as pretended by Robert O. Paxton, historian of Vichy and fascism, in his critique of *The Order of the Day* by Éric Vuillard.[51] This short story, which won its author the Goncourt Prize in 2017, describes two moments in the history of National Socialism. The first, as marginal as it is emblematic, is Hitler's meeting on February 20, 1933, a few weeks after being appointed chancellor, with the elite of German businessmen, twenty-four bankers and industrialists who, after this interview in a dying Reichstag, take out their checkbooks and contribute generously to the financing of the Nazi Party's election campaign. The second is the annexation of Austria, five years later, of which Vuillard tells the sequence of events while recounting a few parallel episodes: first, the dinner of German ambassador Joachim von Ribbentrop at the home of British prime minister Neville Chamberlain, on the evening of the invasion, just before his return to Berlin and his assumption of responsibility for the Reich's Foreign Affairs Ministry; then the last

tête-à-tête between Hitler and Austrian chancellor Kurt Schus-
chnigg, faced with a fait accompli.

Dissatisfied with the fictional reconstruction of these historical events, Paxton criticizes Vuillard for reproducing the
old Marxist cliché of fascism in the pay of big money, recalling
that, apart from a few notable exceptions such as the steel
magnate Fritz Thyssen, the German bourgeoisie was not Nazi,
that it copiously financed all the conservative parties and that
it resigned itself to supporting the Nazi regime only after its
establishment. Vuillard, he argues, would have done better to
more carefully read the historiography of Hitler's rise to power.
Then he observes that, contrary to the narrative proposed by
Vuillard, the UK's attitude to Nazism was the result of a complex set of factors irreducible to Chamberlain's weaknesses,
hesitations, and misunderstandings.

However, Vuillard does not show the Nazis as puppets of
capital. Rather, his striking description of the arrival in the
Reichstag of these *grands bourgeois* focuses on everything that
brought them closer to the old aristocracy. Their style, their
affected manners, and their austere elegance reveal the distance
that separates them from the plebeian matrix of the Nazi movement, but the arguments of Hitler and Göring that promise to
rid them once and for all of communism are very convincing to
their ears. They have no affinity with Nazism, which they did
not create and of which they are wary, but they decide to
support it out of self-interest. Historiography agrees with this
interpretation, of which Vuillard has given a remarkably accurate literary image. Without wishing to summarize a vast

historiographical debate on the relationship between Western democracies and National Socialism, Vuillard convincingly shows that the former were not able to stop the rise of the latter and that, between 1933 and 1939, they are shown to be particularly blind, conciliatory, and often cowardly—from the Spanish Civil War to the invasion of Czechoslovakia, passing precisely through the acceptance of the German annexation of Austria in 1938 and the Munich Conference that followed. It is this weakness and guilty passivity that Chamberlain's silences and indulgence in the face of Ribbentrop's fake and cynical amiability at this London dinner party illustrate in *The Order of the Day.*

Paxton does not like this literary representation of history—that is his right—but the trial he leads against Vuillard is based on a misunderstanding: "Unfortunately," he writes, "we can't tell which parts of the text are his creations, which rely on period archives, and which come from memoirs written in afterthought." Vuillard accumulates a mass of details, he concludes, with the simple aim of showing "history as a spectacle," which "doesn't amount to an explanation."[52] In other words, Paxton criticizes Vuillard for not being a historian, for not approaching the material of his story as a historian, and for not giving it the analytical depth that is required of all historical work. Essentially, it consists of considering history as the exclusive domain of scholars and establishing a hierarchy in which literature would naturally occupy an inferior place. Vuillard is right, in his response, to point out that such a vision relegating literature to an auxiliary and ornamental function is quite simply "retrograde."[53] History is a critical discourse on the past that literature transforms into fiction. Novels try to capture its colors, its atmospheres, its voices, its forms; they dwell on details, which, beyond their seemingly insignificant character, reveal a mental world, the customs, cultures, social relationships of an era. Understanding the past needs both.

■ ■ ■

The controversial question of "historical truth," however, cannot be dismissed in a few words and requires some additional observations. Patrick Boucheron cites Pierre Vidal-Naquet who, at the time of his fight against Holocaust denial, emphasized, with both firmness and humility, a fundamental postulate of historical writing. There is in history, he writes, "something irreducible that, for lack of anything better, I will continue to call the real. In the absence of this real, how can one distinguish the novel from history?"[54] Contrary to the assumptions of partisans of the linguistic turn, the facts in which historians are interested do not have a purely discursive existence, as they are linked to an extratextual reality; this reality is verifiable, and the knowledge that results from it is based on evidential proofs that are not linguistic artifacts.[55] It is certainly true that, in order to exist, facts must necessarily pass through their transcription into language, but they are not invented by language. Since the new historical novel claims its anchoring in history and draws on a wealth of acquired knowledge, its creation should not contradict this. If one wants to make Karski a literary hero, one can shape his personality and attribute invented words to him, but one should not put words in his mouth that contradict what he actually said or wrote.

The notion of historical truth is complex and cannot be used lightly without the necessary precautions either. For my part, I do not share the ontological skepticism of those who, in the wake of Nietzsche, reject it as a lure, as a set of "metaphors, metonymies, and anthropomorphisms," which, after having lent themselves to multiple rhetorical uses, reveal themselves as illusions.[56] We know that this position was taken up by Michel Foucault in a famous essay on Nietzsche and history, and it had already been defended, from 1967, by Roland Barthes, in an essay that would play a certain role in the emergence of the linguistic turn and would mark his desire to take leave of history, "a great empty superego."[57] This posture, which was once one of the flags of postmodernist historiography, has today been abandoned by the majority of scholars. Since antiquity, history has been a search for truth, a quest for and production of knowledge, even if, in each era, the means of elaboration and the criteria for validating this truth may vary.[58] This epistemological relativism problematizes the notion of truth without evacuating it, as one of the tasks of the historiographical operation still consists in sorting out what is true and what is false. Hermeneutics reminds us of this ever since the demonstration by Lorenzo Valla in 1440 that the Donation of Constantine—the document by which the Emperor Constantine granted a third of his empire to the Church of Rome—was apocryphal,[59] and historiography reaffirmed this more recently, notably during the battle led by Pierre Vidal-Naquet and other historians against

Holocaust deniers. To claim that the gas chambers did not exist is a lie.

Literature itself has echoed this distinction between right and wrong, at least since *J'accuse!* by Zola, who denounced the fabrication of the lie on which the accusation against Captain Dreyfus was based. "The truth is on the march, and nothing will stop it": this passage from *J'accuse!* became the slogan of the Dreyfus campaign. Today even supporters of "literary truth" cannot avoid recourse to a quite conventional definition of historical truth. The real hero of *The Impostor*, the "novel" by Javier Cercas, is an unknown historian from the general public, Benito Bermejo, who proved that Enric Marco, the president of the Spanish Association of Former Deportees of Mauthausen, was lying, as he had never been deported.[60] If this notion of what is "true" is the only one recognized (shared as much by history as by literature), that of "literary truth" appears to be much more problematic, since its only criterion of validation resides in the intention of the author. There is no "literary truth" parallel or alternative to that of history. There is a historical reality—a set of proven facts and events—that may constitute the basis of literary creation. Fiction that transgresses historical facts—for example, many literary and filmic uchronias—may certainly stimulate or question understanding of the past, but it does not establish any new truth susceptible to replacement of or juxtaposition with historical truth. The latter, for its part, establishes facts that are always the object of different interpretations.

Undoubtedly, we can challenge the "facto-graphic illusion" of historiographic positivism that postulates a truth immediately contained in its sources,[61] deposited in the archives and ready to be collected and exposed, and we may admit that facts are "constructed" by historians themselves, often after having emerged in a thousand ways within the public space, as well as through the media, the dominant discourse, or, in contrast, through subversive and fragmentary words pronounced by witnesses. But this "fabrication" must be done from given materials. In their investigation of Henri Vidal, "the killer of women" at the start of the twentieth century, Philippe Artières and Dominique Kalifa underscore that, confronted with such a character, the historian sees "the very notion of reality wavering in favor of a shimmering of entangled or stratified, convergent or divergent representations, but whose specter alone draws the complexity, and therefore the truth, of the social world."[62] However, they do not want to abdicate a "demand for truth" for anything and immediately add that "discourse, language, and more generally the archive are not sufficient to restore the full depth of life."[63] The real that shapes history is not the fruit of a tree ready to be picked, but it remains the essential foundation of all historical discourse.

Novelist and literary historian Gabriele Pedullà distinguishes between history and fiction with the help of philology. Historians and novelists share what the classics called *elocutio* (the style and lexical construction of the text) and *dispositio* (the rhetorical structuring of discourse), but they do not have the same approach to *inventio*, which the first practice in its etymological sense (in Latin, *inventio* means "to find") and the others in its modern sense of inventing. The historical imagination is not of the same nature as the novelistic imagination.[64] This distinction is essential for defining the very function of history that, according to Ginzburg, consists in "untangling the strands of the true, the false, and the fictional which are the substance of our being in the world."[65] But, even though historical narration and literary fiction differ, both possess cognitive implications. If they have a connection to truth, this truth is the same.

The novel breaks free from the real: Max Aue did not exist, nor did his reports written for Himmler; Karski's retrospective reflections or Roosevelt's bored yawns are invented by Haenel; Mussolini's erotic fantasies come from Scurati's pen; and Ribbentrop's jokes at Chamberlain's home are a figment of Vuillard's imagination. Still, the tension between exploitation and extermination has really sparked debates within the Reichssicherheitshauptamt (Reich Security Main Office, RSHA) of Oswald Pohl for whom Aue works in *The Kindly Ones*. The list of historiographical controversies is inexhaustible: the attitude of the Allies to the extermination of the Jews and their decision not to bomb Nazi camps continues to be studied by scholars; Mussolini's body is a theme explored by a significant number of works; historians still discuss the rhythm of the European crisis during the 1930s, which was set by Nazi Germany, while the United Kingdom lagged behind; and they also make hypotheses about Ribbentrop, a polyglot from an aristocratic military family: was he the most appropriate, despite his incomprehension of British foreign policy, to play the diplomat's pantomime?

The novels of Littell, Haenel, Scurati, and Vuillard break free from reality to answer, in a fictional mode, a set of questions that historians may address in terms of hypotheses and interpretations. Littell's novel incorporates decades of historiographical investigations on Nazism—the relationship between the "Shoah by bullets" and industrial extermination in the death camps; the culture and mentality of the executioners; the hierarchical relationships within the system of Nazi power—which nourish, well beyond the chronology, events, and historical circumstances evoked, the account of the adventures of its hero. These considerations could be extended to the novelistic portrait of Mussolini by Scurati, who assimilated in depth the historiographical achievements on the symbolic dimension of fascism, the role played by violence in his rise, his "nationalization of the masses," the sources and the forms of his charismatic leadership, the singular mix between tradition and the avant-garde, and the revolution of the right that he acomplished. Over the past thirty years, most historians have agreed to define fascism as a deeply syncretic political movement and ideology. Mussolini, writes Scurati, referring to the birth of fascism in 1919, "insists on what the fascists are not: they are not republicans, socialists, democrats, conservatives, nationalists. They are, on the other hand, a synthesis of all affirmations and negations. We fascists, he concludes, do not have pre-constituted ideas, our doctrine is the fact."[66]

Novels invent characters and situations, but if they break free from the real, with which they establish much more complex relationships than those of simple mimetic reproduction, that does not mean they are lying. They proceed by their own means in search of a deeper and more nuanced understanding of reality. Instead of formulating hypotheses, they construct plots, deploy imaginary situations, scrutinize the psychology of their characters, and explore their mental landscape, as much intellectual as emotional. By moving away from the real, writes Justo Serna, fiction dares to reveal, behind the scenes, the "gray zones," the most hidden and cruel secrets.[67] The new subjectivist historiography, for its part, offers a different answer to the questions posed by these novels: it does not emancipate itself from reality, but reintroduces *storytelling* by sliding it from the actors of the past to the investigator-narrator, the historian firmly established in the present.

Boucheron himself was confronted by the temptation to fill in the blanks of history with fiction. One of his books deals with the missed meeting—or probable but unknown, because if it took place it left no trace—between Leonardo da Vinci and Machiavelli. Contemporaries, they both worked, Leonardo as a military engineer and Machiavelli as a diplomat, with César Borgia, who submitted to them his plan to divert the Arno to the fortification of Florence. In 1502, they were both in Urbino, but no document, neither Leonardo's diary nor Machiavelli's dispatches to the Signoria of Florence, attest to their meeting. After having noted the "intimate complicity between two worlds, two dreams, two ambitions,"[68] Boucheron was obliged to ratify the observation already made, long before him, by the Italian historian Edmondo Solmi: "Places speak, but their occupants are silent."[69] He will therefore not invent any fictional encounter between Leonardo and Machiavelli, for his role consists in questioning this void rather than filling it through his imagination. And it is in a very literary form that he draws this conclusion, by mobilizing two metaphors. History is not (or is not only) a puzzle waiting to be recomposed, as "nothing proves that what lies broken was one day whole, that these isolated words come from one and the same sentence, these shards torn from the bedrock of a single intrigue."[70] To the image of the puzzle, he prefers that of the ford, "a ford to cross to follow the course of a common concern." A ford, because the sources with which historians work are "like the stones of a stream, which we must nevertheless ford, skipping from one to the other."[71] His plea for the "fragility of history"—a history conscious of its limits, of the fact that its knowledge is always an approximation—therefore leads him, after having recognized the fruitfulness of a dialogue between history and literature, to re-establish the frontiers, to conclude that "the literary temptation of the historian is an admission of weakness."[72]

Carlo Ginzburg had already said this in explaining that the narrative choice of microhistory primarily concerns description of the investigation, the way in which the historian explores his sources and constructs a cognitive process:

> Tolstoy leaps over the inevitable gap between the fragmentary and distorted traces of an event (a battle, for instance) and the event itself. But this leap, this direct contact with reality, can take place only on the terrain of invention. It is precluded by definition from the historian, who has at his disposal only fragments of things and documents. The historiographical frescoes that seek to communicate to the reader, through frequently mediocre expedients, the illusion of a vanished reality, tacitly remove this constituent limitation of the historical vocation.[73]

In their modern forms, we have seen, autobiography, novel, and history flourish almost simultaneously at the end of the eighteenth century. Although bridges between these different genres have always existed, a kind of division of labor has emerged empirically. History restored facts and proposed an interpretation, according to a cognitive device that could certainly undergo profound transformations—the transition from the chronological reconstruction of the past to its understanding as a problem—without being substantially called into question. The novel invented characters who brought the past to life with its individual dilemmas and its web of affects, while autobiography opened a window on singular experience, with a subjectivity anchored in an established and verifiable reality. Thus, when Carl Emil Schorske outlines the profile of the Viennese intellectual world at the apogee of the Habsburg Empire, he knows that Stefan Zweig recounted his anguish and chagrin at the time of its dissolution in 1918 and that Joseph Roth painted it as a grandiose epic by narrating the life of the young officer Charles-Joseph von Trotta, the hero of *Radetzky March*. Raul Hilberg, Arno J. Mayer, and Saul Friedländer trace the genesis and unfolding of the Holocaust by questioning its place in history, while Primo Levi gives literary form to the lived experience of its victims. Sheila Fitzpatrick conceptualizes Soviet history knowing that the tragic experience of World War II was already recorded in literature by Vasily Grossman. When he was about to write a history of France in the nineteenth century, Maurice Agulhon knew that the imagination of his future readers was already filled with the fictional figures created by Balzac, Flaubert, Stendhal, and Hugo.

This division of labor has not disappeared, but the borders have become much more porous. Audiovisual creation is probably the place in which the scrambling of tracks is most pronounced thanks to docufiction: those films in which archival material and interviews with specialists of an era, an event, or a historical figure mingle, without a break in continuity, with fictions in which film actors play the role of the heroes of the past during noteworthy episodes of their existence. To appear more interesting and engaging, history must take the form of fiction. The "assault on the border" concerns writers as well as historians: the first construct fictions grafted onto history, built on real historical figures; the second want to introduce into historical narration an emotional dimension that has always belonged to the domain of literature. This is not, however, a simple mixing of roles. The subjectivity at stake in many fictions and historical works is no longer that of the actors of the past but rather of the novelists and historians themselves who revisit the past. It has changed sides. Sebald, Cercas, Jablonka, Artières, and Luzzatto are the true heroes of their works and thus forge an eminently *presentist* relationship with the past. It is no longer just a question of reviving history—according to the ambition of Michelet or Lanzmann—but of transmitting the experiences of the writer and the historian who, in the present, recount history.

Chapter Eight

PRESENTISM

WE MUST now formulate some hypotheses on the origins of the subjectivist turn studied here. Its most visible and striking dimension, as we have seen, is narrative: a literary inflection that, without calling into question the conventional distinction between history and fiction, globally modifies their relationship by injecting into the first several stylistic codes, beginning with homodiegetic narrative, that traditionally belong to the second. The separation between history and novel is therefore blurred by a new interaction that creates quasi-symbiotic forms: while novelists draw more and more inspiration from history and show a considerable concern for factual veracity, historians begin to recount their investigations using the tools of the novel, with plots and heroes who are, in most cases, the authors themselves. Antoine Compagnon, who has always played the role of "double agent" between the two disciplines, perceives in this mutation a "symptom of the state of uncertainty" in which they find themselves today, groping for new identities.[1]

Jablonka, one of the most self-reflective of the proponents of this turn, says it is not about making history books more readable, less boring, or better written by delivering them in a novelistic style. His plea for a meeting between history and literature is not—or is much more—than a simple appeal to historians so that they finally learn to write, instead of contenting themselves with gathering data collected in the archives and ordering it around a few concepts. He pleads for a transition from discourse to text and for an authentic fusion between research and creation; he wishes to inject "epistemology into writing." This is his project:

> If we consider history to be an investigation, and historians investigators driven by a problem, we can then *draw the literary consequences of our method*: using the "I" to situate one's approach and perspective, telling the story of the investigation as well as its "results," going back and forth between the past and the present to which we belong, using emotion as a tool for a better understanding, placing the cursor at the right spot between distance and empathy, choosing the right words, and allowing for the languages that the investigator usually does not share with the people (living or dead) that he or she encounters.[2]

This passionate plea is appealing, but we should question the modalities of this encounter between history and literature around the "I" of the author. From Alessandro Manzoni to

Stendhal, from Leo Tolstoy to Thomas Mann, from Joseph Roth to Vassili Grossman, literature has painted grandiose historical frescoes through the prism of a few individual destinies, a trend continued today, in different forms, by authors such as Jonathan Littell or Antonio Scurati. Many historians seem to follow the opposite path: from large paintings to details, from great history to personal journeys. They do not opt for microhistory, as Carlo Ginzburg and Giovanni Levi practice it, or the historical anthropology of Alain Corbin, both of which go from the particular to the general and who, by investigating a detail, reconstruct the genesis of a historical process to understand the origins of a culture, a society, and an era. Rather, these historians go from the general to the particular or from global history to individual chronicle. They are fiercely attached to sources and depict real historical figures, but they have given up on the big picture: their stories and questions are exhausted in a tale of singular lives enclosed within themselves.

If the subjectivist writing of history undoubtedly constitutes a sizable methodological innovation, it would probably be wrong to consider it a rupture. It marks a turning point in the evolution of a discipline that has known others; it enriches and diversifies it without, however, disrupting it. It would be an exaggeration to compare its effects with the caesura marked by the artistic avant-gardes of the beginning of the twentieth century who, in painting, decomposed perspective with cubism and abolished the laws of figuration with abstraction or who, in music, freed themselves from the laws of harmony to move toward atonal composition. Subjectivist historical writing does not revolt against the institutions that oversee research either;

its supporters are not the Dadaists or the Surrealists of writings of the past. They are, for the most part, respectable scholars well established in academia, where they occupy solid positions. Contained within the anthropological and cultural frameworks of our time, their practice is by no means subversive. On the scientific level, their innovations cannot be considered, a priori, as an advance nor as regression: they explore new avenues whose results are variable and very diverse, spread over a very broad spectrum that brings together as many heirs of Braudel as of Foucault. It is therefore not a question of attributing a political posture to them or of putting them in a school. Subjectivist writing of the past goes across disciplines and political sensibilities and brings together scholars who otherwise have little in common. Rather than catalog them in a school or subdiscipline, this book aims to situate them in their time.

The roots of this subjectivist turn are multiple: some are due to dynamics specific to the historiographical field and others to changes in the contemporary world. It is particularly the latter that will hold my attention here. Of course, it is not wrong to see this shift from a third- to a first-person narration as a symptom of the major changes that affected the humanities, and especially historiography, during the second half of the twentieth century. We must begin by taking into account the influence of sociology and anthropology, which provided historians with techniques of investigation and "participant observation."[3] It has been decades since sociologists of the Chicago School proved the implication of the researcher in his object of investigation.[4] In *Tristes Tropiques* (1955), Claude Lévi-Strauss showed how critical reflection on the premises of a discipline may take the form of an autobiographical narrative.[5] Other changes, often marked by acrimonious debate, are more recent. The linguistic turn, mentioned earlier, transformed the relationship between history and literature and favored the emergence of memory—individual and collective—in the public sphere, a phenomenon that has deeply shaken historiography. After Roland Barthes and Michel de Certeau reminded historians that writing of the past is a textual construction,[6] it is postmodernism that, by questioning the "metanarratives" of modernity, broke the framework of historical epistemology by creating a fragmented gaze. Much more than an ancient teleology that has long been jeopardized, it is the principle of the intelligibility of the past—the diachronic reconstruction of a social totality—that has been replaced by the study of a constellation of subjects atomized on an identity quest.

We must pause for a moment on this mutation, which reverses well-consolidated trends. Reinhart Koselleck uses the concept of *Sattelzeit* (which can be translated as "saddle time" or "transitional epoch") to define the period from the Old Regime to the Restoration. It is during this time, when a dynastic system gives way to a new form of legitimacy based on the idea of nation and a society of orders is supplanted by a society of individuals, that the idea of progress appeared: the cyclical representation of time was dethroned by a linear and ascending vision. The words change meaning and then crystallize a new definition of history as a "singular collective," encompassing both an "event complex" and a unifying narrative, a "historical science."[7] We thus pass from a plurality of narratives (*historie*) to a category capable of bringing together all the experiences of the past: History with a capital *H* (what the Germans call *Geschichte*). The premise of this new "singular collective" is the emergence of an awareness of the historical dialectic that, linking the past as well as the future in a continuous process, has its own semantics emanating from an underlying signification, from a deep and comprehensible meaning. History does not necessarily have telos, but it is still a movement toward the future. Of course, historicism—especially in its positivist versions—has long been aimed at by critics and questioned, but it was not until the advent of a new *Sattelzeit*, at the end of the twentieth century, that History breaks down, that its dialectic evaporates—there is no longer a visible "horizon of expectation"—and that its unity becomes indecipherable. We have witnessed, in recent years, a sort of return to *historie*, a mosaic of the past composed of a thousand fragments, the great historicist river dissolved into a multitude of streams, a labyrinth of singular narratives. The grain of history grows as the big picture blurs; the dilation of details renders the sequence incomprehensible. New subjectivist writing of history is one of the symptoms of this backward *Sattelzeit*.

These intellectual debates have undoubtedly created some of the premises for the subjectivist turn in question here, although this does not necessarily imply filiation or direct influence. The causes of this change, however, are probably more profound and lie in social and cultural transformations of our time that far transcend the internal dynamics of a discipline. We must return here to the hypothesis put forward at the outset: subjectivist historical writing cannot be dissociated from the advent of individualism as one of the major features of the new world order.

First of all, by a spasmodic process of "acceleration," which, with its successive technological innovations, upsets the rhythms of life and compresses social temporalities, neoliberalism has annihilated certain forms of expression of intellectual subjectivity that seemed to us, until recently, timeless.[8] Indeed, within a few years, the Internet, cell phones, and tablets put an end to letter writing, which, for centuries, was the privileged place where writers, thinkers, and researchers allowed themselves to write in the first person. Correspondence has always been the counterpoint to their public work, and their letters lifted the veil on a "self" hidden under the printed texts. Once this dialectic between public and private was annihilated, a subjectivity suddenly orphaned and "deprived of a spiritual shelter," one could say with György Lukács,[9] claimed its rights and decided to manifest itself in the only space that remained available, that of the printed (or at least public) text. And the subjectivity of researchers found a new place in scholarly writing. Thus the autobiographical turn compensates for a loss.

Walter Benjamin, who we have seen previously made a point of never writing in the first person in his essays, devoted a large part of his time to writing letters. According to his friend and correspondent Theodor W. Adorno, this daily practice for him came under the "model of ritual."[10] His subjectivity also found accomplished expression in his calligraphy, minuscule and elegant, dense and regular, which required a certain type of paper. His friend Alfred Cohn provided it to him during the Weimar years and even in exile, when he had to abandon his library.[11] Everything seems done, at the age of universal reification, to erase the singularity of writers by standardizing their material means of creation. Benjamin's case is emblematic, but many others could be mentioned. Among historians, there is, for example, the correspondence between Marc Bloch and Lucien Febvre, which shows the hidden side of the *Annales* laboratory and reveals its tears under German occupation.[12] These high places of expression of intellectual subjectivity that were epistolary exchanges have now disappeared. But other aspects of the rise of the subject in the writing of the past are undoubtedly more important.

■ ■ ■

As many critics have shown, neoliberalism is much more than a model of society based on the deregulation of financial flows, the privatization of public services and key economic sectors, the end of the welfare state, and the dizzying increase in social inequalities. It is a worldview or, speaking with Max Weber, "a rational configuration of the social cosmos."[13] Neoliberal reason has established a "way of life," a series of principles that includes generalized competition and the reshaping of social relations according to the rules of the market, but also the transformation of individuals who conceive and lead their lives as businesses. This is what Foucault called a process of "subjection" (*assujettissement*), namely, "the manner in which one ought to form oneself as an ethical subject acting in reference to the prescriptive elements" of a given social order; the modality of self-constitution of social subjects in a world that shapes and structures them (which also implies the possibility of alternative "subjectivations" made up of struggle and resistance contesting the norm).[14] Subjectivist writing of the past corresponds to this new neoliberal *form of life*, which it expresses as much as normative subjection as the search for alternative subjectivations.

According to its classic formulation given by Friedrich Hayek in *The Road to Serfdom* (1943), neoliberalism is much more than a kind of property doctrine. This, of course, remains its foundation, but the ambition is much greater, because it is indeed, writes Hayek, a "philosophy of individualism," which, he hastens to clarify, should not be interpreted as a form of egotism, but rather as recognition that society and history are the product of "individual acts." Human actions are certainly driven by values and not only determined by interests, but these values "can only exist in the minds of individuals." And, Hayek concludes, "It is this recognition of the individual as the ultimate judge of his ends, the belief that as far as possible his own views ought to govern his actions, that forms the essence of the individualist position."[15] This conception is more than questionable, as individuals are not ontological data that precede and govern their relation with others, but it is precisely their relation with others that shapes them as social subjects endowed with their own autonomy of thought and action: not the free will of a timeless and transcendent subject, but the capacity of a historically constituted being to interact with others and to intervene in its environment. From Karl Marx to Pierre Bourdieu, this argument forms the basis for criticism of the "biographical illusion." But neoliberalism is not just a worldview, as it has a performative dimension. It makes individualism an anthropological paradigm, the habitus of our time: the world looks at itself today on the screen of a smartphone that turns it into a selfie. If we consider this habitus as a form of life, a social framework that imposes itself on us and defines the horizon of our existence, this explains the new need to write history as a story of the self in the present and the public's appetite for works of history written in the first person, a narrative model with which everyone may identify.

At the start of the twenty-first century, neoliberalism gave rise to a new regime of historicity that François Hartog describes as "presentist": a perception and representation of time compressed into the present. What are the distinctive features of presentism? First—and this is the fundamental element—the absence of a future.[16] The past no longer announces the future; it no longer contains any promise of redemption; past and future remain encapsulated in an eternal present. Formerly, the role of historians—Michelet had made it his mission—consisted in giving a place to the dead and to think about the future. As for Marxist historiography, it was teleological precisely in that it set out to place the failed revolutions and defeats of the past in an emancipatory perspective. Once this historical dialectic between past and future was challenged, our relationship with the dead changed. Today the dead "do not pass away," and we establish with them a different, melancholic, and deep relationship, as suggested by the historical accounts of Jablonka, the novels of Sebald and Cercas, and many works in the field of psychology.[17]

The other main feature of the presentist historicity regime resides in its depoliticization. New forms of capitalism are gradually erasing social frameworks of memory, breaking down traditional transmission channels, and depriving collective action of all historical reference. Although conveyed by a multitude of social vectors, from commemorations to culture industry, memory is only deposited in an individual, intimate sphere. It is thus reduced to a set of stories, images, and emotions that substitute for reflection and collective action. This depoliticization reinforces another feature of presentism: the reification of the past. The end of transmissible experience generates "realms of memory," an ensemble of sites, objects, images, and symbols that organize the past as a sort of *patrimony*, an inherited property, as if to be preserved in a museum, ready to be turned into a commodity by the culture industry and individually consumed. The past no longer engenders a utopian imagination, as its perception is structured by commodity consumption. In the same way that it privatizes utopias—the future thought of as a program of individual success—neoliberalism tends to privatize the past, making the self both its observatory and its laboratory.

A neoliberal regime of historicity does not necessarily produce a neoliberal historiography, even if some attempts have been made in this direction by certain "organic intellectuals" of finance capital: David Landes explained to us why the West has deserved its wealth; Niall Ferguson, champion of British imperialism, tried to show how much the Renaissance and the French Revolution owe the bank; and William Goetzmann, the latest, rehabilitated historical teleology to demonstrate that, from antiquity to Wall Street, finance constitutes the true *Weltgeist* of history.[18] These attempts, however, remain few in number, because ultimately neoliberalism is indifferent to historical writing; it is much more interested in "rationalizing" the budget of universities and, more particularly, that of humanities departments. Unlike the totalitarian regimes of the twentieth century, it is not obsessed with the desire to dominate the past. It is not trying to manipulate history or to impose an official vision of the past. On the contrary, it copes very well with commemorations, and its individualistic ethos likes to give itself a virtuous facade by celebrating human rights everywhere.

On the other hand, presentism favors the retreat of scholars into the sphere of the intimate: the atrophy of utopian imagination gives a melancholy gaze turned toward a discontinuous past. Politics occupies a secondary place there; it is not evacuated but observed from afar, often with skepticism, as a form of commitment (not necessarily blindness) belonging to a bygone era. The family replaces society as a privileged realm of memory and historical investigation, a sphere populated by ghosts or spirits, that takes shape between the walls of houses, in the photos, letters, identity papers exhumed from drawers and old cardboard boxes.[19] This brings us back to the photos of grandparents, adored but never known by the child turned historian, and the portrait of a young Falangist in uniform hanging on the wall of the dusty living room of a now empty family home. We thus find *patrimony* in the literal sense of the word, that of a good received as an inheritance from ancestors. This phenomenon does not flow directly from neoliberal reason or its values, but it is the fruit of the presentist perception of the past.

New subjectivist historical writing corresponds to the era of the selfie as self-portrait and as a form of communication that, while being completely centered on the self, takes on a universal character through its reified modalities of visibility and consumption. Some researchers even perceive it as a "technology of the self" that would interiorize modern "pastoral" surveillance (benevolent because apparently noncoercive).[20] In *Laëtitia*, Jablonka analyzes the messages posted by his heroine on Facebook and sees them as a reflection of her social world, her culture, and her generation, the expression of an "I" that in reality designates a "we," as Laëtitia, he writes, paraphrasing Sartre in the conclusion of *The Words*, "is a girl of the twenty-first century, made up of everyone, men and women, girls and boys, who can be considered as all and as anyone."[21] This is right, and his work is an excellent demonstration of Marx's thesis that the individual is not a subject who precedes and determines society, but rather a product of social relations; a thesis that Sartre takes up again in the preface to his book on Flaubert, *The Family Idiot*, by presenting him as a *universal singular* who totalizes his society and his time "by reproducing himself in it as singularity."[22]

This definition also applies in a way to historians like Jablonka and Luzzatto and to writers like Sebald, Mendelsohn, and Cercas. If we accept the idea that history is "a contemporary literature," we must see it as a mirror of its time like any literary creation—in this case, a mirror of the beginning of the twenty-first century, the era of neoliberalism, of retreat into the individual sphere. Admittedly, the books of these authors are not interchangeable, as they can be more or less "true," more or less accomplished and convincing, but Boucheron is right when he notes that, beyond its faults and its merits, in the final analysis, a literary work only testifies "to a certain state of contemporary memory."[23] This is also what Laurent Binet thinks, scoffing at the captivating comments that say that the hero of *The Kindly Ones* "rings true because he is the mirror of his age." Not at all, he retorts, he rings true "because he is the mirror of *our* age: a postmodern nihilist, essentially."[24] On closer examination, all these authors take up the different options that public memory offers us today by problematizing and enriching them with an infinite range of emotions and situations: from the civil religion of the Holocaust (Jablonka, Mendelsohn, Haenel) to postideological revisionism (Cercas), passing through nonconformist variants such as antifascism (Luzzatto, Scurati) or even, at the margin, the memory of those left out, coupled with a form of subversive dandyism (Artières). These approaches are not interchangeable, of course, but together they define a memorial and political horizon.

Jablonka recognizes the limits of his empathy with his grandparents and admits the "derisory character" of his wager. After having meticulously pieced together the threads of their existence, he must admit that he "knows nothing." This admission of modesty is, however, immediately counterbalanced by the satisfaction of the work accomplished, which is not insignificant, since the historian's task, he emphasizes, is to "repair the world."[25] However, the means and techniques of "reparation of the world" vary according to the subjects and the period.

This redemptive conception of history is reminiscent of that of Chateaubriand who, in the aftermath of the Napoleonic wars, entrusted the historian with the task of accomplishing "the vengeance of the nations." This idea had a strong impact on several generations, including that of Vidal-Naquet who, as he writes in his memoirs, for a long time found in these words "a reason to live."[26] But now this restorative virtue seems confined to an intimate, almost domestic space: the historian like Aeneas carrying his father on his shoulders. Repairing the world, specifies Jablonka, corresponds to the Hebrew concept of *tikkun olam*,[27] of which he offers us his version: a noble gesture of family *pietas*, nourished by knowledge and literary talent and devoid of messianism. However, for Gershom Scholem, the messianic redemption has a strong apocalyptic dimension,[28] and for Walter Benjamin redemption of the past can only be accomplished by political action that transforms the present: it is this action that, saving the vanquished from forgetting, makes it possible to repair the past by fulfilling its hopes.[29] Reformulated in secular terms, *tikkun olam* consists of interpreting the past in order to change the present; a task that historians certainly cannot accomplish alone, but one in which their work can fully fit. On the other hand, by Jablonka's own admission, his *tikkun olam* does not go beyond the limits of the domestic sphere and remains far removed from the "conspicuous Judeo-Bolshevism" of his grandparents.[30]

The expansion of the self necessarily implies a narrowing of the us. The new subjectivist writings of the past—historian and literary—are often interpreted, including by their authors, as the expression of a work of postmemory born from the desire to reweave continuity after a rupture and therefore linked, as Marianne Hirsch underscores, to the intergenerational transmission of traumatic experience. These writings are certainly the fact of generations born after the rupture of the war, but we could also see them as a mirror of the generation born or grown up after the great wave of collective commitments of the 1960s and 1970s, a generation that was formed during "the great night-mare of the 1980s,"[31] the years, precisely, marked by the end of militancy, the abandonment of the class struggle as a key cat-egory of historical hermeneutics, the emergence of human rights in political discourse, the rise of the memory of the Holocaust, and the emergence of individualism. Apprehended over a long period of time, this generation belongs to a depoliticized age whose cultural boundaries were drawn by a succession of defeats of postwar collective movements. As the visual arts are always a step ahead of written culture, the cinema announced this turning point in the late 1970s. With self-mockery and a rav-aging critical spirit, Nanni Moretti's first film, in 1978, testified to the dawn of a new era. It was called *I Am Self-Sufficient (Sono un autarchico)*. The rebellious page was turned; in the decades to come, it would only be a question of bereaved memories.

Our relationship to time, as demonstrated by Norbert Elias among others,[32] is not aleatory, optative, or purely subjective; it is socially structured. This does not mean that all margin of autonomy is taken away. There are many Marranos' memories, occult and secret, that are transmitted underground as a coun-tercurrent to the dominant order and its ways of life, but the horizon of our time is that of the market society, a fragmented and atomized world. Its identities are individual, they are no longer collective. Its representations of the past and its "utopias"—if we can thus call its forms of inscription in the future—are "privatized." This does not mean that scholars and writers give shape consciously to a neoliberal worldview. Most even do the opposite. Subjectivist historical writing affirms no ideology; it flows from a social inscription that directs the gaze.

The neoliberal world has become our living environment and our observatory. We live, dream, work, and create within a social framework—and a regime of historicity as well—that we have not chosen. The end of the historical dialectic once described by Koselleck—a symbiotic relationship between the past as a "space of experience" and the future as a "horizon of expectation"[33]—has modified the writing practices of the past. In the era of individualism, subjectivity has imposed itself in the historian's workshop.

Presentism is also an epistemological horizon. For many scholars, it has become the foundation of a new autobiographical and intimate historiography. Today, historians find it difficult to study the subjectivity of collective actors, as E. P. Thompson did sixty years ago when he showed that there are no classes "in themselves," that there are no classes without "class consciousness," that classes are not simple socioeconomic entities but living communities shaped by culture, experiences, generational, religious, and gender divides, etc. A quarter of a century ago, at a time when identity politics were in full swing, Eric J. Hobsbawm recalled the universalist vocation of history: "A history which is designed *only* for Jews (or African-Americans, or Greeks, or women, or proletarians, or homosexuals) cannot be good history, though it may be comforting history to those who practice it."[34] Hobsbawm thus drew attention to the retreat into group identities. Today individual subjectivity has become the prism through which to interrogate the past. This trend is linked to the advent of the neoliberal world, in the same way that the historiography of the nineteenth century reflected the rise of national imaginaries and, fifty years later, the structural history of Fernand Braudel, with tectonic movements in demography and economics, echoed the era of Fordist capitalism, production, and mass culture.

Quarrels between different historical schools have often been a powerful stimulus for research, and there have always been many ways of looking at the past, but the fact remains that each era has its own way of writing history. The example of the *History of the Russian Revolution* by Trotsky, cited at the beginning of this book, in chapter 2, was aimed precisely at highlighting this rift created across a century. One of the protagonists of a historical upheaval felt the need to put aside his ego and to write in the third person to recount this event, analyzing it in all its facets, as should be done in a history book. Today scholars write in the first person to talk about moments in the past they have not experienced.

Wars and revolutions, characterized by the eruption of the masses onto the world stage, produce epic narratives in which collective action transcends individual destinies. It is the breath of history that Jules Michelet and Edgar Quinet, Leon Trotsky and Isaac Deutscher, C. L. R. James or, more recently, Adolfo Gilly and Arno J. Mayer attempt to capture. This also applies to conservative historiography, from Edmund Burke and Tocqueville until, not so long ago, François Furet and Ernst Nolte. Whether we support them or not, revolutionary passions demand narratives that can capture their collective dimension, their polyphony (and it is perhaps because their writing is polyphonic that authors like Éric Vuillard are moving away from the subjectivist posture).[35] Generations that have lived through great historical caesuras produce memorialists and historians drawn to monumental frescoes; our societies produce scholars haunted by their forgotten ancestors. Such a posture is only possible in a world—more precisely, what is called the Western world—where the past is no longer perceived as having a living link with the present, but rather as a landscape reified and transformed into a vast assemblage of realms of memory.

This is how the redemption of previously anonymous lives takes on meaning and transgresses the rules of a peaceful visit to a museumlike past. And this is how the great History, with its cataclysms and tragedies, seems more interesting and truer to us if it is told through the prism of the singular lives it has engulfed that risked being forgotten forever. Once the social frameworks that perpetuated its memory are broken down, collective action becomes an object of scholarly analysis rather than a collection of memories, of transmitted practices, cultures, and experiences. Once the utopias of the twentieth century have been stigmatized and their defeat acknowledged, the revolutionaries of Yiddishland cease to be members of a collective movement and become unique and isolated existences, the grandparents we did not have. New subjectivist historical writings also arose from this historical break. Of course, this is not to blame them, but it is best to be aware of it. If this new historiographical method has qualities and attractions—notably its literary dimension—making it a "manifesto for the social sciences" does not fail to arouse some perplexity: it is a way of sticking to the times, which risks neutralizing the critical spirit. One might well, on this point, retain the lesson of Nietzsche and meditate on the considerations of Agamben: "Those who are truly contemporary, who truly belong to their time, are those who neither perfectly coincide with it nor adjust themselves to its demands. They are thus in this sense irrelevant. But precisely because of this condition, precisely through this disconnection and this anachronism, they are more capable than others of perceiving and grasping their own time."[36]

Literature has always interrogated its relationship to truth, while history, through its schools and methodological quarrels, seeks new avenues for exploring and interpreting the past. Summarizing two centuries of theories of knowledge, Michael Löwy proposes the "belvedere allegory." Understanding the past, he says, is not comparable to the image of an object reflected in a mirror, according to an illusion of accuracy cultivated by positivism that equates the social sciences with the observations of the naturalist. Comparing history and aesthetics, the past, according to Löwy, is rather a landscape painted by an artist whose vision will be as broad as if he chose a high observatory.[37]

Nineteenth-century novelists arrived at the conclusion that all observatories offer a lacunary and unsatisfactory view. One inevitably thinks here of the adventures of Fabrice del Dongo in Waterloo. Having barely joined the ranks of the Napoleonic army, he could not stand the noise of battle. The hussars were struck by enemy cannonballs, the field was strewn with corpses; horses waded through mud and blood, sometimes in the bowels of fallen animals and soldiers. The cannon shots, Stendhal continues, produced a "steady and continuous rumble," but it was difficult to tell whether the detonations were near or far. Immersed in the battle, Fabrice "could not understand in the least what was happening."[38] Enlightened by the Stendhalian lesson, Tolstoy tackled the same question in *War and Peace* (1860) by placing Pierre, one of his heroes, before the same dilemma. In Borodino, the latter is looking for a promontory from where he could contemplate the battle, but he remains disappointed. He looks around, and everything is so indistinct that "he could find nothing that quite lived up to his expectations." An immense landscape spreads out before him in which villages, streams, troops, and bivouacs blend so that he could not even "tell our troops from theirs."[39] It is only after the fact, once the battle is over, that it appears to him in its unity.

The allegory of the belvedere would therefore benefit from being nuanced. Siegfried Kracauer, who compared the historian to Orpheus descending into the realm of the dead, preferred a cinematic metaphor. Like the lifeworld (*Lebenswelt*), the historical universe is heterogeneous and chaotic; to put it in order and recompose it, the historian must probe the past, alternating long shots with close-ups that "isolate and magnify some visual detail."[40] The long shot is the method of Arnold Toynbee and Fernand Braudel (taken up today by Jürgen Osterhammel), followers of the *longue durée* and structural history. As for the close-up, it is used by Erwin Panofsky and today by Carlo Ginzburg. The historian works with these two dimensions, which are as spatial as they are temporal. The *chiffonnier*—like the collector—gathers forgotten and abandoned objects, but must give them a place in a whole, otherwise this work remains useless and sterile: the past would always stay a dead continent awaiting "redemption." The transition from macro- to micro-history does not increase knowledge of reality any more than it impoverishes it; it is a "scale games" that allows you to look differently. The enlargement brings out details that cannot be seen in a long shot, but it fails to encompass the global causes and dynamics, as Jacques Revel demonstrated when analyzing Michelangelo Antonioni's *Blow-Up*. The close-up neglects large collective entities to focus on small movements, singular actors, isolating their actions and questioning their choices. He shows us a humanity "seen from below," "at ground level."[41] But microhistory seizes a detail to trace the chain of historical process and shed light on the entire process; it only makes sense if, by connecting clues from the start, it makes it possible to retrace a path.

The belvedere allegory does not cut between macro- and microhistory. It admits both, as the highest point of view it assumes is a social observatory: the dominated see further or clearer, both near and far, because their vision is critical; they are not interested in defending the established order and rather seek to grasp its contradictions, the hidden mechanisms; their gaze is strategic and their critique is not content with a purely contemplative posture. The vanquished, Koselleck suggested, have a critical mind and observant capacity sharpened by defeat.[42] Their gaze encompasses macro- and microhistory; history from the perspective of the vanquished is made of long-shot tableaus—the industrial revolution painted by E. P. Thompson—and research on a smaller scale: letters from soldiers of the Great War or the "little voices" of Indigenous revolt hidden in British colonial archives.[43] There is no normative approach; historiography is made up of a plurality of currents which apprehend the complexity of the past through different methods, and quarrels between or within disciplines can be as sterile as they are fruitful. Thus it would be unfair and wrong to contest the legitimacy of new subjectivist historical writings. They reflect the sensibility of our time and may give interesting results, provided that their authors are aware of their limits, that they use their ego as a telescope and not as a monad, that they expand the horizon of the subject instead of contracting it down to the "ground level" of an impasse. The subjectivist writing of the past must consider the dilemmas that run through litera- ture and the games of scale that shape historiography. If it does not make the effort to fit individual destinies into a larger his- torical drama, it will not escape from its impasse. We may write history by illuminating its margins and by giving a face to its actors, especially the anonymous people who made it, but we may not interpret the past by simply bringing it back to the realm of the intimate.

The reader will have understood, at least I hope, that this book does not stand *against* these new writings of history, but that it questions the *why* of their appearance. It is not about denying them legitimacy or attributes. The results of this writ- ing are sometimes remarkable, sometimes questionable, in par- ticular because of the risks to which its hermeneutics inevitably expose it. The principal of these dangers consists of locking our- selves in the presentist steel cage that suffocates us instead of removing the bars. After having explored the richness of the horizons opened by the deployment of our multiple "I"—of position, investigation, or emotion—we must not forget that history is above all made of and by "we."

AFRICAN AMERICAN EPILOGUE

With a few exceptions, the historical and literary sources of these chapters come from continental Europe (they are mostly French, with several German, Italian, and Spanish incursions). I had already finished the original version when I discovered the powerful work of Saidiya Hartman. At first glance, *Lose Your Mother* (2007) perfectly conforms to the tropes of subjectivist history: she writes in first person; her book is based on extensive historical documentation without inventing or fictionalizing anything; she describes the steps of her investigation, giving her work a significant autobiographical dimension; she does not hide the emotions related to her discoveries and thoughts; she puts forward the subjective part of her inquiry, admitting how much it is fueled by an identity quest, well expressed by genealogical references and family recollections; finally, her book is built on a twofold historical temporality that merges the reconstitution of the past with an account from the perspective of the present. The history of slavery and the slave trade intermingles with the description of a one-year investigation conducted in Ghana, and this continuous switch between past and present is supported by a remarkable narrative rhythm. Readers do not face a grandiose historical fresco à la Braudel, but rather a literary, historical, and political work in the style of Susan Sontag, even if Hartman combines many skills of both. Undoubtedly, all these elements give Hartman a distinguished place in the constellation of subjectivist authors analyzed in this book, beside someone like Jablonka. Nonetheless, there is something in her writing that overcomes the limits—or avoids the traps—of most subjectivist history.

The main difference is as simple as it is essential. Differently from those of many European historians analyzed in these pages, Hartman's investigation is not confined to a subjective sphere: it transcends the author's self and results in a collective view of the past (as well as inspiring a collective agency in the present). Her latest book—*Wayward Lives* (2019), a reconstitution of the trajectory of rebellious black women in Philadelphia and New York at the beginning of the twentieth century—persuasively explains this posture. She does not fill the blanks of history with her imagination or literary artifacts; nothing is invented, since all characters and events described in her book truly existed. They are gathered from a multitude of sources that usually encumber the historian's workshop and fuel archival investigation: "journals of rent collectors; surveys and monographs of sociologists; trial transcripts, slum photographs; reports of vice investigators, social workers, and parole officers; interviews with psychiatrists and psychologists; and prison case files."[44] Her voice intermingles with those of historical actors by creating a polyphony that, although nonfictional, possesses a powerful lyrical strength. As she elucidates in the "note on method" that opens *Wayward Lives*,

> I recreate the voices and use the words of these young women when possible and inhabit the intimate dimensions of their lives. The aim is to convey the sensory experience of the city and to capture the rich landscape of black social life. To this

end, I employ a mode of close narration, a style which places the voice of narrator and character in inseparable relation, so that the vision, language, and rhythms of the wayward shape and arrange the text. The italicized phrases and lines are utterances from the chorus. The story is told from inside the circle.[45]

A similar hermeneutic "I" is at work in *Lose Your Mother*. Retracing the Atlantic slave route, she tries to capture some life fragments of the enslaved people deported to the New World by exploring the realms of their departure. Saidiya—she chose this Swahili first name in her sophomore year of college—claims her African American identity, but in Accra she quickly realizes the precariousness and elusiveness of the concept of "roots" itself. In Ghana, she was an *Obruni* (a stranger) and a "slave baby." Any dream of finding "roots" and feeling "at home" had to be abandoned as romantic illusion. Slavery was an experience of complete dispossession; there is no "homeland" to recover. Frederick Douglass was right to emphasize that "genealogical trees don't flourish among slaves,"[46] and Saidiya's experience proves this assessment. The African roots of African Americans are fabricated and exhibited by cultural industry. More than a legacy of the past, they are an "invented tradition" forged by the Ghanaian Ministry of Tourism with museums, U.S. universities, and some multinational companies like McDonald's (which organizes "McRoots" tours). Slave memory is finally illustrated by brochures in which Ghana's black kids appear disguised as slaves: "Every town or village had an atrocity to promote."[47] There is nothing to be done: in Accra, Saidiya is a stranger even among her university colleagues. For them, she observes, "my self-proclaimed African identity, albeit hyphenated, was fanciful and my Swahili name an amusement. They could hardly manage to say it without snickering."[48]

In fact, the slaves' past is a mystery. Through genealogical research, Saidyia finds traces of her family at the archives of Willemstad, the capital of Curaçao, thus discovering that her known ancestors were all named Virgilio. However, she does not know the origins of her family name, Hartman. "Return" is an illusion. "The sense of not belonging and of being an extraneous element," she concludes, "is at the heart of slavery."[49] Yet she persists in defining herself as African American. This identity is grounded on a memory of suffering, not on ungraspable "roots" or a mythical imaginary home. It is an identity made of a memory of struggles. African Americans did not inherit a past of rootedness or the promise of a recovered homeland. They receive a legacy of struggle and rebellion, and this is their link with the past. Far from being a retreat into the self, this link is a living continuity of collective agency. Saidiya does not try to imagine her ancestors basking in the beautiful glow of an African landscape at sunset, the evening of a ritual celebration. Her visit to the dungeon of Elmina Castle, the Gold Coast fortification that provided the headquarters of the Royal Africa Company, which the British transformed into one of the main slave "warehouses" on the continent at the end of the seventeenth century, and from which five hundred thousand of slaves were deported, is a meaningful experience. Saidiya does not pretend to know what exactly happened there; she is more interested in understanding "what lived on from this history."[50] Dispossession and oppression are not over. As she writes, the inequalities that affect Blacks in terms of lifespan, poverty, and homicide rate rival those of a third-world country. Her purpose, therefore, is not searching for an idealized past, but rather for the "roots" of a still living despair. In some passages worthy of Fanon, she emphasizes that freedom is not a gift—it has to be taken—and that liberation is usually conquered by violence. Without any embellishment, she quotes the "inaugural gesture of revolt" as transcribed by a French planter:

> That unhappy day was the 23rd of November 1733, at three in the morning. Mr Soetman's Negroes, assisted by others, broke down their master's door, while he was sleeping, ordered him to get up, and, after having stripped him naked, forced him to sing and dance. Then, after having run a sword through his body, they cut his head off, cut open his body, and washed themselves in his blood. To this execution, they added that of his daughter Hissing, thirteen years old, by slaughtering her on top of her stepfather's body.[51]

Violence is horrible and ugly, and nonetheless, Fanon stressed, it can both "humanize" and "detoxify."[52] Of course, a romanticized family saga would avoid these kinds of unpleasant descriptions. Javier Cercas, for example, does not depict the atrocities perpetrated by the Falangists during the Spanish Civil War when he sketches the portrait of his great-uncle as an authentic Homeric hero. Saidiya Hartman's book certainly cannot be read as an apology for violence, but it is at the same time far from the current standards of memory catechism and human rights' rhetorical prescriptions. She proves that it is possible to write in the first person avoiding solipsism and connecting one's manifold "I" with the "we" that makes history.

ACKNOWLEDGMENTS

THE OPPORTUNITY to reflect on the questions addressed in this work arose from two conferences in which I participated in recent years. The first took place at Stanford University in 2017, under the direction of Joan Ramon Resina, and was titled "Inscribed Identities: Writing as Self-Realization" (the proceedings have been edited by Joan with Routledge in 2019). My inaugural conference focused on Jean Améry, the most tormented of authors, for whom "every piece of writing, even theoretical, has a background, an autobiographical substrate." The following year, I formulated some of the ideas developed here, at the Fourteenth Congress of the Spanish Contemporary History Association, at the University of Alicante, under the direction of Mónica Moreno-Seco. I would like to thank my two colleagues who gave me these opportunities, as well as Sergio Luzzatto and Jacob Lachat, who organized two workshops at the Universities of Connecticut and Lausanne in which

I discussed my book. The final version of the manuscript owes a lot to the wise advice of Alexandre Sánchez. This enriched American version would not exist without the support of Wendy Lochner, my editor at Columbia University Press, the excellent translation by Adam Schoene, with whom I had a fruitful collaboration, and a careful revision by Susan Pensak. It has also benefited from the valuable suggestions by Thomas W. Dodman, thanks to whom I discovered Saidiya Hartman's work, and Federico Finchelstein, with whom I had many discussions on the meaning and practice of writing history. I am very grateful to all of them.

NOTES

INTRODUCTION

The epigraph is from Victor Serge, *Memoirs of a Revolutionary*, trans. Peter Sedgwick and George Paizis (New York: NYRB Classics, 2012 [1951]), 53.

1. Jeremy D. Popkin, *History, Historians, and Autobiography* (Chicago: University of Chicago Press, 2005); Jaume Aurell, *Theoretical Perspectives on Historians' Autobiographies: From Documentation to Intervention* (London: Routledge, 2016).

2. Pierre Nora, "Histoire et roman: Où passent les frontières?," *Le Débat*, 165 (2011): 9.

3. Edward Gibbon, *Memoirs of My Life* (New York: Funk and Wagnalls, 1966 [1796]); Henry Adams, *The Education of Henry Adams: An Autobiography* (Boston: Houghton Mifflin, 1971 [1918]); Benedetto Croce, *Contributo alla critica di me stesso* (Milan: Adelphi, 1989 [1918]); Friedrich Meinecke, *Erlebtes 1862–1901* (Stuttgart: Koehler, 1964 [1941]), and *Strassburg, Freiburg, Berlin, 1901–1919: Erinnerungen* (Stuttgart: Koehler, 1949), then included in Eberhard Kessel, ed., *Werke*, Bd. 8: *Autobiographische Schriften* (Stuttgart: Koehler, 1969); Eric Hobsbawm, *Interesting Times: A Twentieth-Century Life* (London: Allen Lane, 2002).

4. Eduardo Galeano, *Voices of Time,* trans. Mark Fried (New York: Picador, 2006).

5. Howard Zinn, *You Can't Be Neutral on a Moving Train: A Personal History* (Boston: Beacon, 1994).

6. Jean-Louis Jeannelle, *Écrire ses mémoires au XXᵉ siècle: Déclin et renouveau* (Paris: Gallimard, 2008), 375.

7. Danilo Montaldi, *Autobiografie della leggera. Vagabondi, ex carcerati, ladri, prostitute raccontano la loro vita* (Turin: Einaudi, 2012 [1961]).

8. Jean Norton Cru, *Du témoignage* (Paris: Allia, 1989 [1930]); Antonio Gibelli, *L'officina della guerra: La Grande Guerra e le trasformazioni del mondo mentale* (Turin: Bollati-Boringhieri, 2007), and also, by the same author, *La Grande Guerra degli Italiani: 1915–1918* (Milan: Rizzoli, 2014).

9. See Claude Pennetier and Bernard Pudal, "Écrire son autobiographie (Les autobiographies communistes d'institution, 1931–1939)," *Genèses* 23 (1996): 57–75, and also the essays brought together by the same authors in *Autobiographies, autocritiques, aveux dans le monde communiste* (Paris: Belin, 2002).

10. Mauro Boarelli, *La fabbrica del passato: Autobiografie di militanti comunisti 1945–1956* (Milan: Feltrinelli, 2007).

11. Blaise Pascal, *Pensées and Other Writings*, trans. Honor Levi (New York: Oxford University Press, 1995), 239.

12. "Berlin Chronicle" (1932), in Walter Benjamin, *Selected Writings*, ed. Michael W. Jennings, Howard Leiland, and Gary Smith (Cambridge, Mass.: Belknap, 1999), 2.2:603.

13. Albert Thibaudet, *Gustave Flaubert* (Paris: Gallimard, 1982 [1922]), 87.

14. Paul Valéry, "Stendhal" (1927), cited by Jacques Lecarme and Éliane Lecarme-Tabone, *L'autobiographie* (Paris: Armand Colin, 2004), 12.

15. Ferdinand Brunetière, "La littérature personnelle" (1889), in Charles-Olivier Stiker-Métral, ed., *L'autobiographie* (Paris: Flammarion, 2014), 223.

16. Brunetière, 226.

17. See Jean Rousset, *Narcisse romancier: Essai sur la première personne dans le roman* (Paris: José Corti, 1973); and Linda Hutcheon, *Narcissistic Narrative: The Metafictional Paradox* (Waterloo: Wilfrid Laurier University Press, 2012 [1980]). While Rousset focuses primarily on Baroque literature, Hutcheon strives to develop a typology of contemporary French and Italian literature in light of the concept of narcissism.

18. To my knowledge, only one study to date has been devoted to historian narcissism, considered, however, as a historiographical expression of a collective identity, taking into consideration the case of German

neoconservative historians at the time of the "quarrel of the historians" (*Historikerstreit*) and that of Israeli "revisionist" historians, who questioned the official account of the Arab-Israeli war of 1948. See José Brunner, "Pride and Memory: Nationalism, Narcissism, and the Historians," *History and Memory* 9, nos. 1–2 (1997): 256–300.

19. Sigmund Freud, "On Narcissism" (1914), in *The Complete Psychological Works of Sigmund Freud*, ed. James Strachey (London: Hogarth, 1953), 14:67–102.

20. Herman Melville, *Moby Dick* (Boston: Botolph Society, 1922 [1851]), 9.

21. Max Weber, *The Protestant Ethic and the "Spirit" of Capitalism*, ed. Peter Baehr and Gordon C. Wells (New York: Penguin, 2002 [1905]), 251. On this subject, see Christopher Adair-Toteff, "Max Weber's Notion of Asceticism," *Journal of Classical Sociology* 10, no. 2 (2010): 109–22.

1. WRITING IN THIRD PERSON

1. Nicole Loraux, "Thucydide n'est pas un collègue," *Quaderni di storia*, no. 12 (1980): 60.

2. Thucydides, *The Peloponnesian War*, trans. Martin Hammond (New York: Oxford University Press, 2009), 12.

3. Thucydides, 12.

4. Thucydides, 12. This aspect of Thucydides' writing is emphasized by Moses I. Finley in his introduction to *The Greek Historians: The Essence of Herodotus, Thucydides, Xenophon, Polybius* (New York: Viking, 1977), 8–13.

5. Thucydides, *The Peloponnesian War*, 270. See Luciano Canfora, "L'io narrante degli storici antichi," *Phaos*, no. 3 (2003): 23–36.

6. See Georg G. Iggers, *Historiography in the Twentieth Century: From Scientific Objectivity to the Postmodern Challenge* (Middletown, Conn.: Wesleyan University Press, 1997), 29–30.

7. Pierre Nora, "General Introduction: Between Memory and History," in *Realms of Memory: The Construction of the French Past*, ed. Pierre Nora, trans. Arthur Goldhammer (New York: Columbia University Press, 1996), 1–20. See also Maurice Halbwachs, *The Collective Memory* (New York: Harper, 1980).

8. See Alessandro Portelli, *Storie orali: Racconto, immaginazione, dialogo* (Rome: Donzelli, 2017).

9. Alexis de Tocqueville, *Recollections* (New York: MacMillan, 1896), 9.

10. Jeremy D. Popkin, *History, Historians, and Autobiography* (Chicago: University of Chicago Press, 2005), 285.

11. Charles Péguy, "De la situation faite à l'histoire et à la sociologie dans les temps modernes," *Cahiers de la Quinzaine* 2, no. 3 (1906): 17, quoted in Christophe Prochasson, "Les jeux du 'Je': Aperçus sur la subjectivité de l'historien," *Société et Représentations* 1, no. 13 (2002): 210.

12. Ivan Jablonka, *History Is a Contemporary Literature: Manifesto for the Social Sciences*, trans. Nathan J. Bracher (Ithaca, N.Y.: Cornell University Press, 2014), 284.

13. Jules Michelet, "Prefatory Note," in *History of France*, trans. G. H. Smith (New York: Appleton, 1892); see also Jules Michelet, *The People* (New York: Appleton, 1846), 25.

14. François Hartog, *Le XIXᵉ siècle et l'histoire: Le cas Fustel de Coulanges* (Paris: Seuil, 2001), 9. More recently, Hartog wrote that Michelet "was able to extirpate himself from the time of *chronos* and shift to the time of *kairos* in order to host the dead." See "Temps et contretemps: Barthes, l'Histoire, le Temps," *MLN* 132 (2017): 888.

15. Prochasson, "Les jeux du 'Je,'" 208. See also Lionel Gossman, "Jules Michelet: Histoire nationale, biographie, autobiographie," *Littérature* 102 (1996): 29–54.

16. According to Leopold von Ranke, "empathy" (*Einfühlung*) meant being able to "locate oneself into a given time, adopting the mind of its contemporaries." *Die grossen Mächte* (Göttingen: Vandenhoeck & Ruprecht, 1955), 22; Wilhelm Dilthey, "The Construction of the Historical World in the Human Studies" (1910), in *Selected Writings*, ed. H. P. Rickman (Cambridge: Cambridge University Press, 1976), 170, 211–12.

17. Michel Brix, "Un suicide littéraire: Autobiographie et réalisme chez Gérard de Nerval," *Revue d'histoire littéraire de la France* 115, no. 3 (2015): 559–78.

18. Marcel Proust, *Contre Sainte-Beuve* (Paris: Gallimard, 1971).

19. Jean Starobinski, *Jean-Jacques Rousseau: Transparency and Obstruction*, trans. Arthur Goldhammer (Chicago: Chicago University Press, 1998), 236. This psychological approach inspires Olney's interpretation of autobiographical writing. See James Olney, *Metaphors of Self: The Meaning of Autobiography* (Princeton: Princeton University Press, 1972).

20. Siegfried Kracauer, *History: The Last Things Before the Last*, completed by Paul Oskar Kristeller (Princeton: Markus Wiener, 1995), 79.

21. Kracauer, 178.

22. François Simiand, "Méthode historique et science sociale" (1903), *Annales ESC* 1 (1967): 87. See Sabina Loriga, *Le petit X: De la biographie à l'histoire* (Paris: Seuil, 2010), 48.

23. Fernand Braudel, *La Méditerranée et le monde méditerranéen à l'époque de Philippe* II (Paris: Armand Colin, 1966), 2:520.

24. Louis Althusser, "Reply to John Lewis" (1973), *Essays in Self-Criticism* (London: NLB, 1976), 50–51.

25. Pierre Bourdieu, "The Biographical Illusion," in *Identity: A Reader*, ed. J. Evans, P. Du Gay, and P. Redman (London: Sage, 2000), 304.

2. THE PITFALLS OF OBJECTIVITY

1. Leon Trotsky, *History of the Russian Revolution*, trans. Max Eastman (Chicago: Haymarket, 2008 [1930]), 1:xviii. Similar considerations apply to *L'histoire de la Commune de 1871*, the first historical reconstruction of the Paris Commune, published in 1876 by Prosper-Olivier Lissagaray (Paris: La Découverte, 2004), who was an actor in it, but decided to write his work as a historian rather than as a witness.

2. Trotsky, *History of the Russian Revolution*, 2:738.

3. Winston Churchill, *The Second World War: Triumph and Tragedy* (Boston: Houghton Mifflin, 1953 [1948]), v.

4. See Richard Vinen, "The Poisoned Madeleine: The Autobiographical Turn in Historical Writing," *Journal of Contemporary History* 46, no. 3 (2011): 531–54, 532.

5. Vinen, 533.

6. Quoted in Nicolas Berg, *The Holocaust and the West German Historians: Historical Interpretation and Autobiographical Memory*, trans. Joel Golb (Madison: University of Wisconsin Press, 2015), 194.

7. Martin Broszat and Saul Friedländer, "A Controversy About the Historicization of National Socialism," *New German Critique* 44 (1988): 85–126, 87–90.

8. Broszat and Friedländer, 125.

9. Broszat and Friedländer, 120.

10. Broszat and Friedländer, 92. On this controversy, see my essay "Nazisme: un débat entre Martin Broszat et Saul Friedländer," in *L'histoire comme champ de bataille. Interpréter les violences du XXᵉ siècle* (Paris: La Découverte, 2012), 129–54.

11. Andreas Hillgruber, *Zweierlei Untergang: Die Zerschlagung des deutschen Reiches und das Ende des europäischen Judentums* (Berlin: Siedler, 1986), 24–25.

12. Jürgen Habermas, "A Kind of Settlement of Damages (Apologetic Tendencies)," *New German Critique* 44 (1988): 25–39. Most pieces of this debate are gathered in *Reworking the Past: Hitler, the Holocaust, and the Historians' Debate*, ed. Peter Baldwin (Boston: Beacon, 1990).

13. George L. Mosse, *The Fascist Revolution: Toward a General Theory of Fascism* (New York: H. Fertig, 1999), 41.

14. George L. Mosse, *Confronting History: A Memoir* (Madison: University of Wisconsin Press, 2000), 108–9.

15. Jean-Claude Pressac, *Les crématoires d'Auschwitz: La machinerie du meurtre de masse* (Paris, CNRS, 1993).

16. Pierre Vidal-Naquet, *L'affaire Audin (1957–1989)* (Paris: Minuit, 1989). Emmanuel Macron was the first French president to recognize the responsibility of the army in the death of Maurice Audin.

17. Carlo Ginzburg, *The Judge and the Historian: Marginal Notes on a Late-Twentieth-Century Miscarriage of Justice*, trans. Antony Shugaar (London: Verso, 1999 [1997]).

18. Paulo Mauri, "Se lo storico accusa il giudice," *La Repubblica*, April 4, 1991.

19. Claudio Pavone, *A Civil War: A History of the Italian Resistance*, trans. Peter Levy (London: Verso, 2014 [1990]).

3. EGO-HISTORY

1. Lawrence Stone, "The Revival of Narrative: Reflections on a New Old History," *Past and Present* 85 (1979): 3–24.

2. Pierre Nora, "Introduction," in Pierre Nora, ed., *Essais d'ego-histoire* (Paris: Gallimard, 1987), 5, trans. Stephen Muecke, "Introduction from *Essais d'Ego-histoire*," in *Ngapartji, Ngapartji: In Turn, Ego-Histoire, Europe, and Indigenous Australia*, ed. Vanessa Castejon, Anna Cole, Oliver Haag, and Karen Hugues (Canberra: ANU, 2014), 21.

3. Nora, 7; 22.

4. Nora, 6; 21.

5. Nora, 5; 21.

6. Cited in François Dosse, *Pierre Nora: Homo historicus* (Paris: Perrin, 2011), 393. See also, by the same author, the entry "Ego-histoire" in Claude Gauvard and Jean-François Sirinelli, eds., *Dictionnaire de l'historien* (Paris: Presses universitaires de France, 2015), 210.

7. Georges Duby, *Mes ego-histoires* (Paris: Gallimard, 2015), 23.

8. Georges Duby, *History Continues*, trans. Arthur Goldhammer (Chicago: University of Chicago Press, 1991).

9. Duby, *Mes ego-histoires*, 41.

10. Duby, 41.

11. Duby, 65–6.

12. Voltaire, "Mémoires pour servir à la vie de M. de Voltaire, écrits par lui-même," in *Écrits autobiographiques* (Paris: Flammarion, 2006 [1759]), 80.

13. Duby, *Mes ego-histoires*, 69.

14. Duby, 112.

15. Benedict Anderson, *A Life Beyond Boundaries: A Memoir* (London:Verso, 2018); Saul Friedländer, *Where Memory Leads: My Life* (New York: Other Press, 2016); Peter Gay, *My German Question: Growing Up in Nazi Berlin* (New Haven: Yale University Press, 1999); Eric Hobsbawm, *Interesting Times: A Twentieth-Century Life* (London: Allen Lane, 2002); Walter Laqueur, *Best of Times, Worst of Times: Memoirs of a Political Education* (Waltham, Mass.: Brandeis University Press, 2009); George L. Mosse, *Confronting History: A Memoir* (Madison: University of Wisconsin Press, 2000); Tony Judt, *The Memory Chalet* (London: Penguin, 2011); Paul Veyne, *Et dans l'éternité je ne m'ennuierai pas. Souvenirs* (Paris: Albin Michel, 2014); Eli Zaretsky, "My Life and Psychoanalysis," *American Imago* 73, no. 4 (2016): 451–68.

16. Jaume Aurell, *Theoretical Perspectives on Historians' Autobiographies: From Documentation to Intervention* (London: Routledge, 2015), 131–69.

17. Annie Kriegel, *Ce que j'ai cru comprendre* (Paris: Robert Laffont, 1991); Pierre Vidal-Naquet, *Mémoires*: vol. 1, *La brisure et l'attente 1930–1955*; vol. 2, *Le trouble et la lumière 1955–1998* (Paris: Seuil, 2007).

18. Vidal-Naquet, *Mémoires*, 1:12.

19. Duby, *History Continues*; Geoff Eley, *A Crooked Line: From Cultural History to the History of Society* (Ann Arbor: University of Michigan Press, 2005); Sheila Fitzpatrick, "Revisionnism in Soviet History," *History and Theory* 46, no. 4 (2007): 77–91; Tulio Halperín Donghi, *Testimonio de un observador paticipante: Medio siglo de estudios latinoamericanos en un mundo cambiante* (Buenos Aires: Prometeo, 2014); Raul Hilberg, *The Politics of Memory: The Journey of a Holocaust Historian* (Chicago: Ivan D. Ree, 1996); Dominick LaCapra, "Tropisms of Intellectual History," *Rethinking History* 8, no. 4 (2004): 499–529; Emmanuel Le Roy Ladurie, *Une vie avec l'histoire. Mémoires* (Paris: Tallandier, 2014); Gérard Noiriel, *Penser avec, penser contre: Itinéraire d'un historien* (Paris: Belin, 2001);

Zeev Sternhell, *Histoire et Lumières: Changer le monde par la raison. Entretiens avec Nicolas Weill* (Paris: Albin Michel, 2014).

20. Carl E. Schorske, "The Author: Encountering History," *Thinking with History: Explorations in the Passage to Modernism* (Princeton: Princeton University Press, 1998), 17–34.

21. Eley, *A Crooked Line*, x.

22. Paul Fussell, *Doing Battle: The Making of a Skeptic* (New York: Little, Brown, 1996); Richard Pipes, *Vixi: Memoirs of a Non-Belonger* (New Haven: Yale University Press, 2006); Fritz Stern, *Five Germanys I Have Known: A History and Memoir* (New York: Farrar, Straus and Giroux, 2006).

23. Saul Friedländer, *When Memory Comes*, trans. Helen R. Lane (New York: Farrar, Straus and Giroux, 1979).

24. Anna Bravo, *A colpi di cuore. Storie del sessantotto* (Rome: Laterza, 2008); Giovanni De Luna, *Le ragioni di un decennio 1969–1979: Militanza, violenza, sconfitta, memoria* (Milano: Feltrinelli, 2009); Luisa Passerini, *Autobiography of a Generation: Italy, 1968*, trans. Lisa Erdberg (Hanover, N.H.: Wesleyan University Press, 1996 [1988]); Benjamin Stora, *La dernière génération d'Octobre* (Paris: Stock, 2003). See Joseph Maslen, "Autobiographies of a generation? Carolyn Steedman, Luisa Passerini and the memory of 1968," *Memory Studies* 6, no. 1 (2013): 23–36; and Sheila Rowbotham, *Promise of a Dream: Remembering the Sixties* (London: Allen Lane, 2000).

25. Carolyn Steedman, *Landscape for a Good Woman: A Story of Two Lives* (London: Virago, 1986).

26. Simone de Beauvoir, *Memoirs of a Dutiful Daughter*, trans. James Kirkup (New York: Harper Perennial Modern Classics, 2005); Jean-Paul Sartre, *The Words: The Autobiography of Jean-Paul Sartre*, trans. Bernard Frechtman (New York: Vintage, 1981); Giorgio Agamben, *Autoritratto nello studio* (Rome: Nottetempo, 2017).

27. See, among others, Sidonie Smith and Julia Watson, eds., *Women, Autobiography, Theory: A Reader* (Madison: University of Wisconsin Press, 1998). For a more sociological approach, see Liz Stanley, *The Auto/Biographical I: The Theory and Practice of Feminist Auto/Biography* (Manchester: Manchester University Press, 1995).

28. Luisa Passerini, *Autobiography of a Generation: Italy, 1968* (Hanover, N.H. Wesleyan University Press, 1996).

29. Passerini, 117.

30. Passerini, 118. On this subject, see Derek Duncan, "Corporeal Histories: The Autobiographical Bodies of Luisa Passerini," *Modern Language Review* 93, no. 2 (1998): 370–83.

31. The notion of "ego-historical plural" is suggested by Luisa Passerini in her review of Joan W. Scott's *The Fantasy of Feminist History* (2011) in *Gender and History* 25, no. 2 (2013): 388–89.

32. Jeremy D. Popkin, *History, Historians, and Autobiography* (Chicago: University of Chicago Press, 2005), 122.

33. Nicolaus Sombart, *Jugend in Berlin 1933–1943: Ein Bericht* (Frankfurt: Fischer, 1991), *Pariser Lehrjahre 1951–1954: Leçons de sociologie* (Hamburg: Hoffmann und Campe, 1994).

34. Jürgen Kuczynski, *Memoiren: Die Erziehung des J. K. zum Kommunisten und Wissenschaftler* (Berlin: Aufbau, 1975); Hans Mayer, *Der Turm von Babel: Erinnerung an eine Deutsche Demokratische Republik* (Frankfurt: Suhrkamp, 1991). One could also mention Sebastian Haffner, *Geschichte eines Deutschen: Die Erinnerungen 1914–1933* (Munich: Deutsche Verlags-Anstalt, 2000).

35. Gaetano Salvemini, *Dai ricordi di un fuoruscito* (Turin: Bollati Boringhieri, 2002 [1960]). Among Italian historian autobiographies, one should mention Mario Isnenghi, *Vite vissute e no: I luoghi dell amia memoria* (Bologna: Il Mulino, 2020). In Spain, Aurell recently put together fifteen historian autobiographies, but it is interesting to note that the only text by a contemporary specialist is that of an Irish historian, Mary Nash. See Jaume Aurell, ed., *La historia de España en primera persona: Autobiografías de historiadores hispanistas* (Barcelona: Base, 2012).

36. See Giovanni Miccoli, *Delio Cantimori: La ricerca di una nuova critica storiografica* (Turin: Einaudi, 1997); Carlos Forcadell, "Semblanza biográfica de Juan José Carreras Ares," in Juan José Careras Ares, *Lecciones sobre Historia* (Saragoza: Institución Fernando el Católico, 2016), 19–36; Pedro Ruiz Torres, "Josep Fontana en su tiempo," *Ayer* 116, no. 4 (2019): 307–23.

37. Eric J. Hobsbawm, *The Age of Extremes: The Short Twentieth Century, 1914–1991* (New York: Vintage, 1994), ix.

38. Hobsbawm, 5.

39. François Furet, *The Passing of an Illusion: The Idea of Communism in the Twentieth Century* (Chicago: University of Chicago Press, 1999), xi.

40. Fussell, *Doing Battle*, and, also by Paul Fussell, *The Great War and Modern Memory* (New York: Oxford University Press, 1975).

41. Omer Bartov, *Hitler's Army: Soldiers, Nazis, and War in the Third Reich* (New York: Oxford University Press, 1992), viii.
42. Saul Friedländer, *Nazi Germany and the Jews: The Years of Persecution, 1933–1939* (New York: Harper Collins, 2007), xxv–xxvi.
43. Saul Friedländer, "Trauma, Transference, and 'Working Through' in Writing the History of the Shoah," *History and Memory* 4, no. 1 (1992): 39–59.

4. SHORT INVENTORY OF "I" NARRATIVES

1. Pierre Birnbaum, *La leçon de Vichy: Une histoire personnelle* (Paris: Seuil, 2019), 70.
2. Birnbaum, 71.
3. See, in particular, Pierre Birnbaum, *Un mythe politique: La "république juive" de Léon Blum à Pierre Mendès France* (Paris: Fayard, 1988), and, by the same author, *The Jews of the Republic: A Political History of State Jews in France from Gambetta to Vichy*, trans. Jane Todd (Stanford: Stanford University Press, 1996).
4. Birnbaum, *La leçon de Vichy*, 110. See Michael R. Marrus and Robert O. Paxton, *Vichy France and the Jews* (Stanford: Stanford University Press, 2019 [1981]).
5. Birnbaum, *La leçon de Vichy*, 228.
6. Mona Ozouf, *Composition française: Retour sur une enfance bretonne* (Paris: Gallimard, 2009), 148.
7. Michel Winock, *Jeanne et les siens* (Paris, Seuil, 2003).
8. Stéphane Audoin-Rouzeau, *Quelle histoire: Un récit de filiation (1914–2014)* (Paris: EHESS/Gallimard/Seuil, 2013), 13 and 140.
9. Maurice Olender, *Un fantôme dans la bibliothèque* (Paris: Seuil, 2017), 63.
10. Ivan Jablonka, *A History of the Grandparents I Never Had*, trans. Jane Kuntz (Stanford: Stanford University Press, 2016), xiii.
11. Jablonka, xiii.
12. Ivan Jablonka, *Laëtitia* (Paris: Seuil, 2016).
13. Jablonka, 72.
14. Jablonka, 8.
15. Ivan Jablonka, *En camping-car* (Paris: Seuil, 2018), 153.
16. Philippe Artières, ed., *Le livre des vies coupables: Autobiographies de criminels 1896–1909* (Paris: Albin Michel, 2000).

17. Philippe Artières and Dominique Kalifa, *Vidal, le tueur de femmes: Une biographie sociale* (Lagrasse: Verdier, 2017 [2001]).
18. Philippe Artières, *Vie et mort de Paul Gény* (Paris: Seuil, 2013), and, by the same author, *Au fond* (Paris: Seuil, 2016).
19. Teixeira has noted two illustrious antecedents of this stylistic process in *Life of Jesus* by Ernest Renan (1863) and the "Monologue with Freud" that concludes *Freud's Moses: Judaism Terminable and Interminable* (1993) by Josef Hayim Yerushalmi. See Luis Teixeira, "À la recherche de Paul Gény," *Écrire l'histoire*, nos. 13–14 (2014): 179–82.
20. Artières, *Vie et mort de Paul Gény*, 60.
21. Artières, 109.
22. Philippe Artières, *Reconstitution: Jeux d'histoire* (Paris: Manuella, 2013). The playful use of archives was already asserted in *Vidal, le tueur de femmes*, 20. According to Alexander Cook, who, however, does not reject the principle, one of the main limitations of *reenactment* is "a persistent tendency to privilege a visceral, emotional engagement with the past at the expense of a more analytical treatment." See Alexander Cook, "The Use and Abuse of Historical Reenactment: Thoughts on Recent Trends in Public History," *Criticism* 46, no. 3 (2004): 490.
23. Ivan Jablonka, "Quand l'histoire nous traverse: Entretien avec Philippe Artières," *La vie des idées*, June 7, 2014.
24. Artières, *Vie et mort de Paul Gény*, 217.
25. Artières, 184.
26. Laurent Demanze, *Un nouvel âge de l'enquête* (Paris: José Corti, 2019), 145.
27. As Dominique Viart writes in *Vie et mort de Paul Gény*, "the text draws the narrator subject or even the author himself in the infinite vertigo of his questioning, even to make the author the character of a narrative that was originally intended to be objective and distant." See Dominique Viart, "Incohérences narratives du fait divers," in Matteo Majorano, ed., *L'incoerenza creativa nella narrativa francese contemporanea* (Macerata: Quodlibet, 2016), 99–113.
28. Antoine de Baecque, *La traversée des Alpes: Essai d'histoire marchée* (Paris: Gallimard, 2018 [2014]).
29. De Baecque, 36 and 129.
30. De Baecque, 38.
31. De Baecque, 62–63.
32. De Baecque, 56.
33. De Baecque, 542.

34. Primo Levy, *The Periodic Table* (1975), trans. Ann Goldstein, in *The Complete Works of Primo Levi* (New York: Liveright, 2017), 2:860.

35. Sergio Luzzatto, trans. Frederika Randall, *Primo Levi's Resistance: Rebels and Collaborators in Occupied Italy* (New York: Metropolitan Books, 2016).

36. On the distinction between the different stages of the Italian Resistance, cf. Santo Peli, *La Resistenza in Italia: Storia e critica* (Turin: Einaudi, 2004). Claudio Pavone devoted a chapter to the "punitive system" within the partisan movement, *A Civil War: A History of the Italian Resistance* (London: Verso, 2014 [1990]), chapter 7.

37. Luzzatto, *Primo Levi's Resistance*, 31–32.

38. Mark Mazower, *What You Did Not Tell: A Russian Past and the Journey Home* (New York: Other Press, 2017).

39. Omer Bartov, *Anatomy of a Genocide: The Life and Death of a Town Called Buczacz* (New York: Simon and Schuster, 2018), 299.

40. Artières, *Au fond*, 33.

41. Jablonka, *A History of the Grandparents I Never Had*, 98.

42. Carlo Ginzburg, "Clues: Roots of an Evidential Paradigm," in *Clues, Myths, and the Historical Method*, trans. John and Anne C. Tedeschi (Baltimore: Johns Hopkins University Press, 1989), 87–112.

43. Ivan Jablonka, trans. Nathan J. Bracher, *History Is a Contemporary Literature: Manifesto for the Social Sciences* (Ithaca, N.Y.: Cornell University Press, 2018), 248.

44. Jablonka, *A History of the Grandparents I Never Had*, 211. On the distinction between literature and fiction in Jablonka, see Dominick LaCapra, "What Is History? What Is Literature?," *History and Theory* 56, no. 1 (2017): 99.

45. See Laurent Demanze, "Les enquêtes d'Ivan Jablonka: Entre histoire et littérature," *Les Temps Modernes* 692 (2017): 196.

46. Max Weber, *The Methodology of the Social Sciences*, trans. Edward A. Shils and Henry A. Finch (Glencoe, Ill.: Free Press, 1949). Notably, see the essay on the meaning of "ethical neutrality in sociology and economics."

47. Wolf Lepenies, *Between Literature and Science: The Rise of Sociology*, trans. R. J. Hollingdale (Cambridge: Cambridge University Press, 1988).

48. Jean-Claude Passeron, "L'illusion du monde réel:—graphie,—logie,—nomie," in C. Grignon and J.-C. Passeron, *Le savant et le populaire: Misérabilisme et populisme en sociologie et en littérature* (Paris: Gallimard/Seuil, 1989), 249.

49. Claude Lévi-Strauss, "Les limites de la notion de structure en ethnologie" (1972), cited in François Hartog, *Évidences de l'histoire: Ce que voient les historiens* (Paris: EHESS, 2005), 113.

50. Claude Lévi-Strauss, *The Naked Man,* trans. John and Doreen Weightman (New York: Harper and Row, 1981), 687.

51. Richard Hoggart, *A Local Habitation* (London: Chatto and Windus, 1988), 30.

52. Pierre Bourdieu, *Sketch for a Self-Analysis,* trans. Richard Nice (Chicago: University of Chicago Press, 2008).

53. Didier Eribon, *Returning to Reims,* trans. Michael Lucey (Los Angeles: Semiotext(e), 2013).

54. Eribon, 25.

55. Eribon, 100.

56. Eribon.

57. Nathalie Heinich, *Une histoire de France: Récit* (Paris: Les Impressions nouvelles, 2018).

58. Heinich, 218

59. Heinich, 219

60. See Norbert Elias and John L. Scotson, *The Established and the Outsiders: A Sociological Enquiry Into Community Problems* (London: Frank Cass, 1965).

61. Elias and Scotson, 221.

62. Nicole Lapierre, *Le silence de la mémoire: À la recherche des Juifs de Plock* (Paris: Plon, 1989).

63. Nicole Lapierre, *Changer de nom* (Paris: Gallimard, 2006 [1995]), and, by the same author, *Causes communes* (Paris: Stock, 2011).

64. Nicole Lapierre, *Sauve qui peut la vie* (Paris: Seuil, 2015).

65. Lapierre, 249.

66. Nicole Lapierre, "Éloge de la bâtardise," interview with Ivan Jablonka, *La vie des idées*, May 28, 2010.

67. See Michel Warschawski, *On the Border,* trans. Levi Laub (London: Pluto, 2005); Benjamin Stora, *La dernière génération d'Octobre* (Paris: Stock, 2003); Daniel Bensaïd, *An Impatient Life: A Memoir,* trans. David Fernbach, foreword by Tariq Ali (London: Verso, 2014); Régine Robin, *Berlin chantiers* (Paris, Stock, 2001).

5. DISCOURSE ON METHOD

1. Ivan Jablonka, *History Is a Contemporary Literature: Manifesto for the Social Sciences,* trans. Nathan J. Bracher (Ithaca, N.Y.: Cornell University Press, 2018), 208–9.

2. Jablonka, 242. See also Nathan Bracher, "Timely Representations: Writing the Past in the First-Person Present Imperfect," *History and Memory*

28, no. 1 (2016): 3–35; and Dominick LaCapra, "What Is History? What Is Literature?," *History and Theory* 56, no. 1 (2017): 98–113.

3. Jablonka, *History Is a Contemporary Literature*, 178. This is why one could establish Jablonka as a "writer à la Perec." See Laurent Demanze, "Les enquêtes d'Ivan Jablonka entre histoire et littérature," *Les Temps modernes*, no. 692 (2017): 192–203.

4. This is particularly evident in the quote drawn from *History of the French Revolution*, which Jablonka highlights in his own *A History of the Grandparents I Never Had*.

5. Paul Ricœur, *Time and Narrative*, trans. Kathleen McLaughlin and David Pellauer (Chicago: University of Chicago Press, 1984); see also Paul Ricœur, "Narrative Identity," *Philosophy Today* 35, no. 1 (1991): 73–81.

6. Jablonka, *History Is a Contemporary Literature*, 242–45.

7. See Bracher, "Timely Representations," 32.

8. Ivan Jablonka, *Laëtitia* (Paris: Seuil, 2016), 224.

9. Jablonka, 357.

10. Philippe Artières, "Ivan Jablonka, l'histoire n'est pas une littérature contemporaine!," *Libération*, November 6, 2016. A defense of Jablonka is found in Nathan Bracher, "Jablonka et la question du sujet en sciences sociales: Le cas de *Laëtitia ou la fin des hommes*," *French Politics, Culture, and Society* 36, no. 3 (2018): 92–108.

11. Léonore Le Caisne, "Laëtitia ou la fin de l'enquête scientifique," *Revue d'histoire moderne et contemporaine* 64, no. 1 (2017): 175–85.

12. Enrico Mattioda, "À propos de l'édition française de Partigia de Sergio Luzzatto," *Laboratoire italien* 18 (2016): 4. For a defense of Luzzatto's method, see Marcello Flores, "Une polémique sur les intentions cachées," *Atelier international de recherche sur les usages publics du passé*, May 18, 2013.

13. Carlos Forcadell, "Historia social: De la clase a la identidad," in Elena Hernández Sandonica and Alicia Langa, eds., *Sobre la historia actual: Entre política y cultura* (Madrid: Abada, 2005), 16–35.

14. Fernand Braudel, "Histoire et sciences sociales: La longue durée," in *Écrits sur l'histoire* (Paris: Flammarion, 1969), 12.

15. Christopher A. Bayly, *The Birth of the Modern World, 1780–1914: Global Connections and Comparisons* (Malden, Mass.: Blackwell 2004); Jürgen Osterhammel, *The Transformation of the World: A Global History of the Nineteenth-Century* (Princeton: Princeton University Press, 2016); Ian Kershaw, *To Hell and Back: Europe, 1919–1949* (New York: Viking, 2015), and *The Global Age: Europe, 1949–2017* (New York: Viking, 2018).

16. See, for example, Mark Mazower, *Dark Continent: Europe's Twentieth Century* (New York: Knopf, 1999), and, by the same author, *Hitler's Empire: How the Nazis Ruled Europe* (London: Penguin, 2009).

17. Philippe Artières, *La banderole: Histoire d'un objet politique* (Paris: Autrement, 2013), and, by the same author, *La police de l'écriture: L'invention de la délinquance graphique 1852–1945* (Paris: La Découverte, 2013).

18. See Philippe Lejeune, "The Autobiographical Pact," in *On Autobiography*, ed. Paul John Eakin (Minneapolis: University of Minnesota Press, 1989), 5.

19. Lejeune, 22.

20. Patrick Boucheron and Mathieu Riboulet, *Prendre dates: Paris, 6 janvier–14 janvier 2015* (Lagrasse: Verdier, 2015).

21. Boucheron and Riboulet, 8, 7.

22. Catherine Calvet, "Patrick Boucheron et Mathieu Riboulet: 'La question aujourd'hui est 'qui est nous?' plutôt que 'qui est Charlie?,'" *Libération*, July 10, 2015.

23. Boucheron and Riboulet, *Prendre dates*, 49.

24. Boucheron and Riboulet, 60.

25. Boucheron and Riboulet, 114.

26. Emmanuel Todd, *Who Is Charlie?: Xenophobia and the New Middle Class* (Cambridge: Polity, 2016).

27. Nicolas Vieillescazes, "Qu'est-ce qu'un intellectuel d'ambiance?," *Lundi matin* 189, April 29, 2019.

28. Houria Bouteldja, "Mohamed Merah et moi," *Indigènes de la République*, April 6, 2012.

6. MODELS

1. Esther Benbassa, *Suffering as Identity: The Jewish Paradigm* (London: Verso, 2010).

2. Yosef Hayim Yerushalmi, *Zakhor: Jewish History and Jewish Memory* (Seattle: University of Washington Press, 1996 [1982]); Pierre Nora, ed., *Realms of Memory: The Construction of the French Past*, trans. Arthur Goldhammer (New York: Columbia University Press, 1996 [1984]); Primo Levi, *The Drowned and the Saved*, trans. Raymond Rosenthal (New York: Vintage International, 1989 [1986]).

3. Claude Lanzmann, "Hier ist kein warum" (1988), in Stuart Liebman, ed., *Claude Lanzmann's* Shoah*: Key Essays* (New York: Oxford University Press, 2007), 51; see Primo Levi, "If This Is a Man" (1946), trans. Ann

Goldstein, in *The Complete Works of Primo Levi* (New York: Liveright, 2015), 1:25.

4. Lanzmann, "Hier ist kein warum," 489.

5. Shoshana Felman, "In an Era of Testimony: Claude Lanzmann's *Shoah*," *Yale French Studies* 79 (1991): 58.

6. See Dominick LaCapra, "Lanzmann's *Shoah*: 'Here There Is No Why,'" in *History and Memory After Auschwitz* (Ithaca, N.Y.: Cornell University Press, 1998), 100–1.

7. Ivan Jablonka, *History Is a Contemporary Literature: Manifesto for the Social Sciences*, trans. Nathan J. Bracher (Ithaca, N.Y.: Cornell University Press, 2018), 179.

8. Art Spiegelman, *Maus: A Survivor's Tale*, vol. 1: *My Father Bleeds History*, vol. 2: *And Here My Troubles Began* (New York: Pantheon, 1986, 1991).

9. Andreas Huyssen, "Of Mice and Mimesis: Reading Spiegelman with Adorno," *New German Critique*, no. 81 (2000): 65–82. See Max Horkheimer and Theodor W. Adorno, "Elements of Anti-Semitism: Limits of Enlightenment," in *Dialectic of Enlightenment: Philosophical Fragments*, ed. Gunzelin Schmid Noerr, trans. Edmund Jephcott (Stanford: Stanford University Press, 2002), 137–72. On the use of the concept of mimesis in Adorno and Horkheimer, see, above all, Anson Rabinbach, *In the Shadow of Catastrophe: German Intellectuals Between Apocalypse and Enlightenment* (Berkeley: University of California Press, 1997), notably chapter 6, "The Cunning of Unreason: Mimesis and the Construction of Anti-Semitism in Horkheimer and Adorno's *Dialectic of Reason*," 166–97.

10. Spiegelman, *Maus*, 2:41.

11. Spiegelman.

12. Spiegelman, 16. See Rick Iadonisi, "Bleeding History and Owning His [Father's] Story: 'Maus' and Collaborative Autobiography," *CEA Critic* 57, no. 1 (1994): 41–56.

13. Sergio Luzzatto, *Max Fox o le relazioni pericolose* (Turin: Einaudi, 2018), 250.

14. Luzzatto, 250; Javier Cercas, *The Impostor: A True Story*, trans. Frank Wynne (New York: Knopf, 2018); Emmanuel Carrère, *Limonov*, trans. John Lambert (New York: Farrar, Straus and Giroux, 2014).

15. W. G. Sebald, *The Emigrants*, trans. Michael Hulse (New York: New Directions, 1996), *The Rings of Saturn*, trans. Michael Hulse (New York: New Directions, 1998), *Austerlitz*, trans. Anthea Bell (New York: Random House, 2002).

16. See Laura Martin, "Reading the Individual: The Ethics of Narration in the Works of W. G. Sebald as an Example for Comparative Literature," *Comparative Critical Studies* 11, no. 1 (2014): 40.

17. Mark M. Anderson, "The Edge of Darkness: On W. G. Sebald," *October,* no. 106 (2003): 102–21.

18. W. G. Sebald, *Vertigo,* trans. Michael Hulse (New York: New Directions, 1999).

19. Sebald, *The Emigrants,* 181.

20. Patrick Modiano, *Dora Bruder,* trans. Joanna Kilmartin (Berkeley: University of California Press, 1999).

21. Susan Weiner, "Dora Bruder and the 'Longue Durée,'" *Studies in Twentieth- and Twenty-First-Century Literature* 31, no. 2 (2007): 403–14.

22. Modiano, *Dora Bruder,* 63–64.

23. See Susan R. Suleiman, " 'Oneself as Another': Identification and Mourning in Patrick Modiano's *Dora Bruder,*" *Studies in Twentieth- and Twenty-First-Century Literature* 31, no. 2 (2007): 325–50. She refers to the concept of "empathetic identification," elaborated by Paul Ricœur, *Oneself as Another,* trans. Kathleen Blamey (Chicago: University of Chicago Press, 1992).

24. Patrick Modiano, *Honeymoon,* trans. Barbara Wright (London: Harvill, 1992). For a comparison between these two works, see Claude-Pierre Pérez, "Imaginer sur pièces: Imagination et documentation chez Patrick Boucheron et Patrick Modiano," *Littérature* 190, no. 2 (2018): 106; and especially Michaël Sheringham, "Le dispositif *Voyage de noces-Dora Bruder,*" in Roger-Yves Roche, ed., *Lectures de Modiano* (Nantes: Cécile Defaut, 2009), 251.

25. Daniel Mendelsohn, *The Lost: A Search for Six of Six Million* (New York: HarperCollins, 2006).

26. Mendelsohn, 522.

27. Mendelsohn, 653.

7. HISTORY AND FICTION

1. Umberto Eco, *The Name of the Rose,* trans. William Weaver (New York: Everyman's Library, 2006). See, notably, Alessandra Fagioli, "Il romanziere e lo storico: Intervista a Umberto Eco," *Lettera internazionale,* no. 75 (2003).

2. Jonathan Littell, *The Kindly Ones: A Novel*, trans. Charlotte Mandell (New York: Harper, 2009).

3. Yannick Haenel, *The Messenger: A Novel*, trans. Ian Monk (Berkeley: Counterpoint, 2012).

4. Javier Cercas, *Soldiers of Salamis: A Novel*, trans. Anne McLean (New York: Bloomsbury, 2005); *Lord of All the Dead*, trans. Anne McLean (New York: Knopf, 2020).

5. Hans Magnus Enzensberger, *The Silences of Hammerstein: A German Story*, trans. Martin Chalmers (New York: Seagull, 2009).

6. Antonio Scurati, *M. Il figlio del secolo* (Milan: Bompiani), 2018.

7. Scurati, 4.

8. Littell, *The Kindly Ones*, 13–6.

9. Littell, 664. The critics of this novel, even the most severe, have recognized the extent of its documentation. Stressing that the strength of the book lies in its "skillful combination" and its "rare alliance of history and fiction," Antoine Compagnon insists on the precision of the historical setting reconstituted by Littell: "I was not unaware of it because the press signaled it, but I was nevertheless surprised to note that almost everything was there: the names, the facts, the words. You think the characters are made up, but no, Littell makes them do what they did and say what they said." See Antoine Compagnon, "Nazisme, histoire et féérie: Retour sur *Les Bienveillantes*," *Critique*, no. 726 (2007): 881–96.

10. See, along with the novels of Haenel and Scurati already cited, Leonardo Padura, *The Man Who Loved Dogs: A Novel*, trans. Anna Kushner (New York: Farrar, Straus and Giroux, 2014).

11. Ivan Jablonka, *A History of the Grandparents I Never Had*, trans. Jane Kuntz (Stanford: Stanford University Press, 2016), 211.

12. Jablonka, 285.

13. Laurent Binet, *HHhH*, trans. Sam Taylor (New York: Farrar, Straus and Giroux, 2012), 17–18.

14. Binet, 241.

15. Binet, 127–28.

16. Binet, 178.

17. Christine Berberich, "'I think I'm beginning to understand. What I'm writing is an *infranovel*': Laurent Binet, *HHhH* and the Problem of 'Writing History,'" *Holocaust Studies* 25, nos. 1–2 (2018): 74–87, 79.

18. Cercas, *Lord of All the Dead*, 262–63.

19. Cercas, 142.

20. Cercas, 212.

21. Cercas, 212–13.

22. Siegfried Kracauer, "Photography" (1927), in *The Mass Ornament: Weimar Essays*, trans. Thomas Y. Levin (Cambridge, Mass.: Harvard University Press, 1995), 56.

23. Cercas, *Lord of All the Dead*, 257.

24. See David Becerra Mayor, "La Guerra Civil en la literatura Española actual: Entre el consenso de la transición y el consenso neoliberal," *Revista Chilena de Literatura* 98 (2018): 73–103; Raquel Macciuci, "Apuntes sobre posmemoria para leer *El monarca de las sombras* de Javier Cercas," *Pasajes* 56 (2019): 41–59.

25. Dominick LaCapra, "Historical and Literary Approches to the Final Solution: Saul Friedländer and Jonathan Littel," in Dominick LaCapra, *History, Literature, and Critical Theory* (Ithaca, N.Y.: Cornell University Press, 2013), 105. According to Littell, in *The Kindly Ones,* the narratorial "I" functions as a "he," thus reintroducing the necessary critical distance of the narrative. See Jonathan Littell and Pierre Nora, "Conversation sur l'histoire et le roman," *Le Débat* 144 (2007): 29. He thus establishes with his hero a relationship of "heteropathic identification." On this concept, see Dominick LaCapra, *Writing History, Writing Trauma* (Baltimore: John Hopkins University Press, 2014), 40.

26. Justo Serna, *Historia y ficción: Conversaciones con Javier Cercas* (Madrid: Punto de Vista, 2019), 241.

27. Serna, 244–45.

28. Serna, 211–12. See also Fabien Escalona and Lise Wajeman, "Javier Cercas, 'Le passé n'est pas passé,'" *Mediapart*, September 14, 2018.

29. Roberto Vivarelli, *La fine di una stagione. Memoria 1943–1945* (Bologna: Il Mulino, 2000), 105–6.

30. Vivarelli, 26.

31. I will mention here, in the field of historiography, the well-known work of Christopher Browning, *Ordinary Men: Reserve Police Battalion 101 and the Final Solution in Poland* (New York: Harper Perennial, 2017); and the biography of the poacher who became SS commander Oskar Dirlewanger by Christian Ingrao, *The SS Dirlewanger Brigade: The History of the Black Hunters*, trans. Phoebe Green (New York: Skyhorse, 2011). In sociology, see especially Harald Welzer and Michaela Christ, *Täter: Wie aus ganz normalen Menschen Massenmörder warden* (Frankfurt: Fischer, 2005). On the literary level, see Bernhard Schlink, *The Reader*, trans. Carol Brown Janeway (New York: Vintage, 2008).

32. Serna, *Historia y ficción*, 11. On the question of historical revisionism (including Nolte and De Felice), see chapter 5 of my book *The New Faces of Fascism: Populism and the Far Right* (London: Verso, 2019), 131–50.

33. Serna, *Historia y ficción*, 118.

34. On Spanish historiographical revisionism, see especially Ricardo Robledo, "El giro ideológico en la historia contemporánea española: 'Tanto o más culpable fueron las izquierdas,'" in Carlos Forcadell, Ignacio Peiró, and Mercedes Yusta, eds., *El pasado en construcción: Revisiones de la historia y revisionismos históricos en la historiografía contemporánea* (Zaragoza: Institución Fernando el Católico, 2015), 303–38.

35. On Violante's speech, see Filippo Focardi, *La guerra della memoria: La Resistenza nel dibattito politico italiano dal 1945 a oggi* (Bari: Laterza, 2005).

36. Javier Cercas, *The Anatomy of a Moment: Thirty-Five Minutes in History and Imagination*, trans. Anne McLean (New York: Bloomsbury, 2011), 15. In an essay on literature, he underscores that the structure of his book is that of a novel. See Javier Cercas, *The Blind Spot: An Essay on the Novel*, trans. Anne McLean (London: MacLehose, 2018), 30.

37. Jan Karski, *Story of a Secret State: My Report to the World* (Washington, D.C.: Georgetown University Press, 2013).

38. Haenel, *The Messenger*, 113.

39. Haenel, 117.

40. Haenel, 113.

41. See Antoine Compagnon, "Histoire et littérature, symptôme de la crise des disciplines," *Le Débat* 165 (2011): 69.

42. Quoted by Patrick Boucheron, who makes it the title of his own reflections on the subject, "Toute littérature est assaut contre la frontière: Notes sur les embarras historiens d'une rentrée littéraire," *Annales* 65, no. 2 (2010): 451.

43. Claude Lanzmann, "*Jan Karski* de Yannick Haenel: un faux roman," *Les Temps modernes* 657 (2010): 1.

44. See Manuel Braganca, "Faire parler les morts: sur Jan Karski et la controverse Lanzmann-Haenel," *Modern and Contemporary France* 23, no. 1 (2015): 35–46.

45. Annette Wieviorka, "Faux témoignage," *L'Histoire* 349 (2010): 30.

46. George Steiner, *The Portage to San Cristóbal of A. H.* (New York: Simon and Schuster, 1981).

47. See Edouard Husson and Michel Terestchenko, *Les complaisantes: Jonathan Littell et l'écriture du mal* (Paris: François-Xavier de Guibert, 2007),

which calls for censorship against *The Kindly Ones*, and Ernesto Galli della Loggia, "'M' di Antonio Scurati: Il romanzo che ritocca la storia," *Il Corriere della Sera*, October 13, 2018. On the historian debate around *The Kindly Ones*, see Jean Solchany, "Les Bienveillantes ou l'histoire à l'épreuve de la fiction," *Revue d'histoire moderne et contemporaine* 54, no. 3 (2007): 178.

48. Solchany, 178.

49. Solchany, 165. See the interview with Jonathan Littell in *Le Monde*, November 17, 2006.

50. See the violent charge by Galli della Loggia, "'M' di Antonio Scurati;" and Antonio Scurati's response, "Scurati replica a Galli della Loggia: Raccontare è arte, non scienza esatta," *Il Corriere della Sera*, October 17, 2018.

51. Éric Vuillard, *The Order of the Day*, trans. Mark Polizzotti (New York: Other Press, 2018).

52. Robert O. Paxton, "The Reich in Medias Res," *New York Review of Books*, December 6, 2018.

53. Éric Vuillard, "Novels as History," *New York Review of Books*, February 7, 2019.

54. Pierre Vidal-Naquet, "Lettre," in Luce Giard, ed., *Michel de Certeau* (Paris: Center Georges Pompidou, 1987), 71–72. Quoted in Patrick Boucheron, "Toute littérature est assaut contre la frontière," 465. See also Pierre Vidal-Naquet, *Assassins of Memory: Essays on the Denial of the Holocaust*, trans. Jeffrey Mehlman (New York: Columbia University Press, 1992). It is the same conclusion drawn—from the point of view of literary theory—by Käte Hamburger, *The Logic of Literature*, trans. Marilynn J. Rose (Bloomington: Indiana University Press, 1973), which reminds us that, unlike history where it is real people who pronounce words, in the novel it is words that invent people (203). I contextualized this passage from Vidal-Naquet in my essay, *Le passé, modes d'emploi: Histoire, mémoire, politique* (Paris: La Fabrique, 2005), 67–69.

55. See Roger Chartier, *On the Edge of the Cliff: History, Language, and Practices*, trans. Lydia G. Cochrane (Baltimore: Johns Hopkins University Press, 1997), 18–20; and Richard J. Evans, *In Defense of History* (New York: W. W. Norton, 1999), 95-97, 107-108.

56. Friedrich Nietzsche, "On Truth and Lie in a Nonmoral Sense," in *On Truth and Untruth: Selected Writings*, trans. Taylor Carman (New York: HarperCollins, 2019), 29.

57. Michel Foucault, "Nietzsche, Genealogy, History," in *The Foucault Reader*, ed. Paul Rabinow (New York: Pantheon, 1984); Roland Barthes, "The

Discourse of History," in *The Rustle of Language*, trans. Richard Howard (New York: Hill and Wang, 1986). See François Hartog, "Temps et contretemps: Barthes, l'histoire et le temps," *MLN* 132, no. 4 (2017): 876–89. Among the historians who defend this Foucauldian posture, but by problematizing it and nuancing it to the point of making it interesting and fruitful, there is Joan W. Scott, "History-Writing as Critique," in Keith Jenkins, Sue Morgan, and Alun Munslow, eds, *Manifestos for History* (London: Routledge, 2007), 19–38.

58. See Carlo Ginzburg, *Threads and Traces: True, False, Fictive*, trans. Anne C. Tedeschi and John Tedeschi (Berkeley: University of California Press, 2012).

59. Ginzburg, chapter 3.

60. Cercas underscores that, even if it occupies a marginal place and intervenes only at the end, the figure of Bermejo is the "authentic hero" of his work. Serna, *Historia y ficción*, 223.

61. See Florent Coste, "Propositions pour une littérature d'investigation," *Journal des anthropologues* 148–49 (2017): 48–49; and Laurent Demanze, *Un nouvel âge de l'enquête: Portraits de l'écrivain contemporain en enquêteur* (Paris: José Corti, 2019), 21.

62. Philippe Artières and Dominique Kalifa, *Vidal, le tueur de femmes: Une biographie sociale* (Lagrasse: Verdier, 2017 [2001]), 18.

63. Artières and Kalifa, 19.

64. Gabriele Pedullà, "Carlo Ginzburg, *Il filo e le trace: Vero, falso, finto*," *Laboratoire italien* 7 (2007): 5.

65. Ginzburg, *Threads and Traces*, 6.

66. Scurati, *M*, 112. On the relationship of Scurati's novel to the historiography of fascism, see the excellent development of Maddalena Carli, "Le fascisme en prise directe: Autour du dernier roman d'Antonio Scurati, *M. Il figlio del secolo*," *Politika*, May 6, 2019.

67. Serna, *Historia y ficción*, 55.

68. Patrick Boucheron, *Léonard et Machiavel* (Lagrasse: Verdier, 2008), 24.

69. Boucheron, 17.

70. Boucheron, 82.

71. Boucheron, 79.

72. Patrick Boucheron, "On nomme littérature la fragilité de l'histoire," *Le Débat* 165, no. 3 (2011): 55. In the same issue of the review, Alain Corbin agrees with Boucheron on this point, stressing that "to take the path of fictional, epic, or romantic literature is to submit writing to an aesthetic

project which does not correspond to the aim of the historian." See Alain
Corbin, "Les historiens et la fiction: Usages, tentation, nécessité . . .," *Le
Débat* 165, no. 3 (2011): 60.

73. Ginzburg, *Threads and Traces*, 209.

8. PRESENTISM

1. Antoine Compagnon, "Histoire et littérature, symptôme de la crise des
   disciplines," *Le Débat*, no. 165 (2011): 62–70.
2. Ivan Jablonka, *History Is a Contemporary Literature: Manifesto for the Social
   Sciences*, trans. Nathan J. Bracher (Ithaca, N.Y.: Cornell University Press,
   2018), viii.
3. The notion belongs to Polish ethnologist Bronisław Malinowski, *Argo-
   nauts of the Western Pacific* (London: Routledge and Kegan Paul, 1922).
4. See, for example, Nels Anderson, *The Hobo: The Sociology of the Homeless
   Man* (Chicago: University of Chicago Press, 1961); William Foote Whyte,
   Street Corner Society: The Social Structure of an Italian Slum (Chicago: University of Chicago Press, 1961).
5. Claude Lévi-Strauss, *Tristes tropiques*, trans. John and Doreen Weightman (New York: Penguin, 1992).
6. Roland Barthes, "The Discourse of History," in *The Rustle of Language*,
   trans. Richard Howard (New York: Hill and Wang, 1986).
7. On the emergence of a new conception of history, see Reinhart
   Koselleck, *The Practice of Conceptual History: Timing History, Spacing
   Concepts*, trans. Todd Samuel Presner (Stanford: Stanford University
   Press, 2002). On the notion of *Sattelzeit*, see Reinhart Koselleck's introduction to his monumental work on historical concepts, coedited with
   Otto Brunner and Werner Conze, *Geschichtliche Grundbegriffe: Histo-
   risches Lexikon zur politisch-sozialen Sprache in Deutschland*, t. 1 (Stuttgart:
   Klett-Cotta, 1972), xv. See, in this regard, Gabriel Motzkin, "On the
   Notion of Historical (Dis)Continuity: Reinhart Koselleck's Construction of the *Sattelzeit*," *Contributions to the History of Concepts* 1, no. 2
   (October 2005): 145–58.
8. See Hartmut Rosa, *Social Acceleration: A New Theory of Modernity*, trans.
   Jonathan Trejo-Mathys (New York: Columbia University Press, 2013).
9. György Lukács, *Soul and Form*, ed. John T. Sanders and Katie Terezakis,
   trans. Anna Bostock (New York: Columbia University Press, 2010).

10. Theodor W. Adorno, "Benjamin the Letter Writer," in *On Walter Benjamin: Critical Essays and Recollections*, ed. Gary Smith (Cambridge, Mass.: MIT Press, 1988).

11. Enzo Traverso, "Adorno and Benjamin: Letters at Midnight in the Century," chapter 6 of *Left-Wing Melancholia: Marxism, History, and Memory* (New York: Columbia University Press, 2016), 178–203.

12. Marc Bloch and Lucien Febvre, *Correspondance*, 3 vols. (Paris: Fayard, 1994–2004).

13. Pierre Dardot and Christian Laval, *The New Way of the World: On Neoliberal Society*, trans. Gregory Elliott (London: Verso, 2017).

14. Michel Foucault, *The History of Sexuality*, vol. 1: *An Introduction* trans. Robert Hurley (New York: Vintage, 1990), 60; Michel Foucault, *The History of Sexuality*, vol. 2: *The Use of Pleasure*, trans. Robert Hurley (New York: Vintage, 1990), 26.

15. Friedrich Hayek, *The Road to Serfdom* (Chicago: University of Chicago Press, 1944), 66.

16. François Hartog, *Regimes of Historicity: Presentism and Experiences of Time*, trans. Saskia Brown (New York: Columbia University Press, 2015).

17. For instance, Magali Molinié, *Soigner les morts pour guérir les vivants* (Paris: Seuil, 2006).

18. David S. Landes, *The Wealth and Poverty of Nations: Why Some Are So Rich and Some So Poor* (New York: Norton, 1999); Niall Ferguson, *The Ascent of Money: A Financial History of the World* (New York: Penguin, 2008); William Goetzmann, *Money Changes Everything: How Finance Made Civilization Possible* (Princeton: Princeton University Press, 2016).

19. Marianne Hirsch, *Family Frames: Photography, Narrative, and Postmemory* (Cambridge: Harvard University Press, 1997).

20. Kimberly Hall, "Selfies and Self-Writing: Cue Card Confessions as Social Media Technologies of the Self," *Television and New Media* 17, no. 3 (2016): 228–42. See Michel Foucault, *Technologies of the Self: A Seminar with Michel Foucault*, ed. Luther H. Martin, Huck Gutman, and Patrick H. Hutton (Amherst: University of Massachusetts Press, 1988).

21. Ivan Jablonka, *Laëtitia* (Paris: Seuil, 2016), 186–87, which refers to Jean-Paul Sartre, *The Words*, trans. Bernard Frechtman (New York: Vintage, 1981).

22. Jean-Paul Sartre, *The Family Idiot: Gustave Flaubert, 1821–1857*, trans. Carol Cosman (Chicago: University of Chicago Press, 1981–1993), 1:ix.

23. Patrick Boucheron, "Toute littérature est assaut contre la frontière: Notes sur les embarras historiens d'une rentrée littéraire," *Annales* 65, no. 2 (2010): 463.

24. Laurent Binet, *HHhH*, trans. Sam Taylor (New York: Farrar, Straus and Giroux, 2012), 240.

25. Ivan Jablonka, *A History of the Grandparents I Never Had*, trans. Jane Kuntz (Stanford: Stanford University Press, 2016), 292.

26. Pierre Vidal-Naquet, *Mémoires*, vol. 1: *La brisure et l'attente 1930–1955* (Paris: Seuil, 2007), 113–14. See Chateaubriand, *Memoirs from Beyond the Tomb*, trans. Robert Baldick (New York: Penguin, 2014), 221.

27. Jablonka, *A History of the Grandparents I Never Had*, 292.

28. Gershom Scholem, *The Messianic Idea in Judaism: And Other Essays on Jewish Spirituality* (New York: Schocken, 1971).

29. Walter Benjamin, "Theses on the Philosophy of History," in *Illuminations*, ed. Hannah Arendt, trans. Henry Zohn (New York: Schocken, 1969).

30. Jablonka, *A History of the Grandparents I Never Had*, 291.

31. François Cusset, *La décennie: Le grand cauchemar des années 1980* (Paris: La Découverte, 2006).

32. Norbert Elias, *Time: An Essay* (Dublin: University College Dublin Press, 2007).

33. Reinhart Koselleck, "'Space of Experience' and 'Horizon of Expectation': Two Historical Categories," in *Futures Past: On the Semantics of Historical Time*, trans. Keith Tribe (New York: Columbia University Press, 2004), 255–75.

34. Eric J. Hobsbawm, "Identity History Is Not Enough," in *On History* (London: Weidenfeld and Nicolson, 1997), 266–77.

35. See, for example, Éric Vuillard, *14 Juillet* (Arles: Actes Sud, 2016), and, by the same author, *The War of the Poor*, trans. Mark Polizzotti (New York: Other Press, 2020).

36. Giorgio Agamben, "What Is the Contemporary?" in *What Is an Apparatus? And Other Essays*, trans. David Kishik and Stefan Pedatella (Stanford: Stanford University Press, 2009), 40.

37. Michael Löwy, *Paysages de la vérité: Introduction à une sociologie critique de la connaissance* (Paris: Anthropos, 1985), 219.

38. Stendhal, *The Charterhouse of Parma*, translated by C. K. Scott Moncrieff (London: New Phoenix Library, 1951), 54.

39. Leo Tolstoy, *War and Peace*, trans. Anthony Briggs (New York: Penguin, 2005), 844–45. See the illuminating essay by Sabina Loriga, "Tolstoï dans le scepticisme de l'histoire," *Esprit*, no. 315 (June 2005): 6–25.

40. Siegfried Kracauer and Paul Oskar Kristeller, *History: The Last Things Before the Last* (Princeton: Wiener, 1995), 105–6. Adopting Kracauer's perspective, the allegory suggested by Mona Ozouf remarking on the limits

of the novelist and the historian, the first myopic, and the second presby-opic, appears questionable. See Mona Ozouf, "Récit des novelistes, récit des historiens," *Le Débat* 165 (2011): 22.

41. Jacques Revel, *Jeux d'échelles: La micro-analyse à l'expérience* (Paris: Gallimard/Seuil, 1996), 12, and also, by the same author, "L'histoire au ras du sol," preface to Giovanni Levi, *Le pouvoir au village: Histoire d'un exor-ciste dans le Piémont du XVIIIe siècle* (Paris: Gallimard, 1989), i–xxxiii.

42. Reinhart Koselleck, "Transformations of Experience and Methodologi-cal Change: A Historical-Anthropological Essay," in *The Practice of Con-ceptual History: Timing History, Spacing Concepts*, 45–83.

43. See, respectively, E. P. Thompson, *The Making of the English Working Class* (New York: Pantheon, 1964); Antonio Gibelli, *L'officina della guerra: La Grande Guerra e le trasformazioni del mondo mentale* (Turin: Bollati-Boringhieri, 2007 [1990]); Ranajit Guha, "The Small Voice of History," *Subaltern Studies* 9 (1996): 1–12.

44. Saidiya Hartman, *Wayward Lives, Beautiful Experiments: Intimate Histo-ries of Riotous Black Girls, Troublesome Women, and Queer Radicals* (New York: Norton, 2019), xiv.

45. Hartman, xiii–iv.

46. Quoted by Saidiya Hartman, *Lose Your Mother: A Journey Along the Atlan-tic Slave Route* (New York: Farrar, Straus and Giroux, 2007), 90–91.

47. Hartman, 163.

48. Hartman, 218.

49. Hartman, 88.

50. Hartman, 130.

51. Hartman, 91–92.

52. Frantz Fanon, *The Wretched of the Earth*, trans. Richard Philcox (New York: Grove, 2004), 44.

INDEX

INDEX

Past, 10, 24, 44–45, 47, 104; future and, 144, 151; history and, 14, 17–18, 154; as impersonal, 12–13; Nazis and, 26–28; presentism and, 145–46, 149. *See also* History
Patrimony, 145, 146
Pavone, Claudio, 31, 178*n*36
Paxton, Robert O., 49, 122, 123, 124
Pedullà, Gabriele, 128
Péguy, Charles, 16, 18
Peloponnesian War, 11–12
People, The (Michelet), 17
People's History of the United States, A (Zinn), 4
Perec, Georges, 78
Periodic Table, The (Levi, P.), 61–62
Perrais, Jessica, 53
Perrais, Laëtitia, 53, 80–81, 82
Perrot, Michelle, 35
Philology, 128
Photography, 19, 112
Photos, in *The Emigrants*, 96
Piacenza, Aldo, 63
Pirandello, Luigi, 19
Pohl, Oswald, 129
Poland, 64, 73–74, 105, 119
Poliakov, Leon, 26
Politics, 51, 146, 151
Popkin, Jeremy D., 3, 15–16, 38
Position, "I" of, 79
Positivism, 16, 35, 80, 154; Durkheim and, 69; historians and, 30; historiographic, 121, 127
Pound, Ezra, 19
Po Valley, 5
Powerlessness, 86, 88
Prendre dates (Boucheron and Riboulet), 85–87

Presentism: African Americans, 158–63; history and literature, 135–37; neoliberalism and, 141, 142–47, 150–51; subjectavist historical writing, 137–40, 142–43, 145–46, 149–51
Pressac, Jean-Claude, 30
Primo Levi's Resistance (Luzzatto), 61–63, 81–82
Prochasson, Christophe, 18
"Prose chroniclers," as truth benders, 11–12
Proust, Marcel, 19, 24
Psychoanalysis, 26, 34, 45, 92–93

"Quarrel of the historians" (*Historikerstreit*), 27–28, 168*n*18
Quelle histoire (Audoin-Rouzeau, S.), 51
Quinet, Edgar, 152

Radetzky March (Roth), 133
Ranke, Leopold von, 13, 18, 170*n*16
Reagan, Ronald, 33
Real, the, 125, 128, 129, 130–31
Realism, 19
Reality, 20, 21, 120, 127, 143
Realms of Memory (Nora), 14, 34–35
Rémond, René, 35
Renan, Ernest, 177*n*19
Returning to Reims (Eribon), 71–72
Revel, Jacques, 156
Revisionism, history and, 116–17
Revue historique (academic journal), 16
Ribbentrop, Joachim von, 122, 124, 129
Riboulet, Mathieu, 85–87